SPIN *to* weave

SPIN *to* weave

THE WEAVER'S GUIDE TO MAKING YARN

Sara Lamb

INTERWEAVE.
interweave.com

EDITOR Ann Budd

TECHNICAL EDITOR Rita Buchanan

PROJECT AND GALLERY PHOTOGRAPHER Joe Coca

PHOTO STYLIST AND SAMPLE PHOTOGRAPHER Ann Swanson

ART DIRECTOR Liz Quan

COVER AND INTERIOR DESIGN Karla Baker

PRODUCTION Katherine Jackson

Interweave Press LLC
A division of F+W Media, Inc.
201 East Fourth Street
Loveland, CO 80537
interweave.com

Manufactured in China by Asia Pacific Offset Ltd.

Library of Congress Cataloging-in-Publication Data

Lamb, Sara, 1951-
   Spin to weave : the weaver's guide to making yarn / Sara Lamb.
      pages cm
   ISBN 978-1-59668-648-9 (pbk.)
   ISBN 978-1-59668-810-0 (PDF)
1. Hand spinning. 2. Yarn. I. Title.
   TT847.L36 2013
   746.1'2--dc23
                              2012046674

10 9 8 7 6 5 4 3 2 1

acknowledgements

A book is not produced alone. Yes, there are many hours of creating and writing before it becomes a collaborative project, but once the team of editors, photographers, and designers steps in, the book truly takes shape. Thank you to Ann and Rita for all of your kind and generous help. Thanks also to Ann Swanson for her good humor, photographic skill, and drawings. I would be remiss in not also thanking Anne Merrow, my first book editor, who started me down this path. Thanks also to the people behind the scenes at Interweave Press who cheer me on, including Amy, Karen, Linda, and Marilyn. You have no idea how grateful I am for the years of support and encouragement.

Spinning can be a very social activity. I so appreciate the exchange of ideas and camaraderie I have found at gatherings of spinners. Words cannot express how much I have learned at these events, and I hope in this small way to return the favor.

Weaving is much more solitary, but we gather together in guilds and at conferences to share, show, teach, and learn. Thanks to every volunteer who ever helped at guilds and fiber conferences—these organizations and activities are the lifeblood that keeps weavers informed and connected. Thank you also to all of the small businesses that make up the fiber marketplace, from farmers and fiber producers, to shops and manufacturers. I have met most of the vendors who make my work possible at conferences—thank you for attending.

Thank you to my friends for your help and advice and to my fellow weavers for your contributions—I am happy to have been able to include some of your work here. Thanks also to my family for understanding my preoccupation with twist and setts these many months.

Thanks most especially to my husband Kurt, who is a true friend and partner in everything I do.

contents

INTRODUCTION
handspun for weaving

I AM A SPINNER WHO WEAVES, which gives me great freedom in my cloth—I have fibers from all over the world at my disposal. In my weaving, I can focus on particular fibers and yarn constructions, how they behave in particular weave structures, and the usefulness and durability of the resulting fabric. I can make any number of textiles, regardless of current fashion or style, and create custom fabrics and yarns for any specific purpose. I find the freedom to spin and weave any textile I imagine to be a great gift, indeed.

WHEN I LEARNED TO WEAVE IN 1976,

I purchased commercial yarns from weaving supply shops. I lived in the city at the time and never considered spinning until I moved to the country the following year. Suddenly, there were no weaving supply shops nearby, but there were plenty of sheep. So, in order to feed my loom, I learned to spin. No one warned me that handspun yarns might not be as durable and resistant to abrasion as commercially spun yarn, and my spinning teachers all happened to be weavers, so it never occurred to me that spinning to weave might be odd or unusual.

Embracing the country life, I decided to raise my own sheep. Each year I washed, carded, and spun their wool for weaving garments and household textiles, such as jackets, blankets, pillows, and rugs. Through trial and error, I learned which types of yarns were best for which purposes, and my yarns began to improve as I observed how they behaved in the textiles I made from them.

Since those days, more people are spinning and weaving cloth from handspun yarns. The fibers available to spinners are more diverse and, although we still can buy fleece directly from the farmers, wonderful preparations are also available, either direct from mills or from independent dyers. With this new abundance, it's time to rethink old ideas and old ways of doing things. The cloth I want to weave now is quite different and more refined, and I've updated the fibers and spinning techniques to match.

I remember years ago having a conversation among spinners about finding inspiration. Many said their ideas started with the fiber—either they raised fiber animals or had bought fiber and needed to find a use for it. The two of us in the group who were weavers agreed that our inspiration began at the other end—the finished object (as in the Tussah Silk Kimono on page 107). If we wanted a skirt, we searched for a fiber that would be appropriate for a skirt; if we wanted a tote bag, we started with a fiber that would make a sturdy bag. Unlike a lot of spinners, my inspiration does not come from the materials I use; rather, the materials are simply the medium. For me, whatever it is that I want to weave sets the parameters for the fiber, twist, grist, color, and all the other choices I make when spinning. I am still inspired by the fibers, and buy small lots, both dyed and undyed, and then plan projects that suit them (see the Alpaca Scarf on page 77). I may not know what I will make with each fiber at the point of purchase, but when I sit down to spin, I have a plan in mind.

I spin almost every day. This means that I make a lot of yarn and, to keep from being overwhelmed by it, I have to use it! I start with a sample and, if it works, I move on to the fabric.

The more fabric I make, the more the fabric ends up being what I want. I am enamored of plain, everyday fabrics—solid fabrics that stand up to use and wear. They are durable and will be around for a long while, so I'd best like them! The fabrics I weave vary according to fiber choice and grist, and I can make them in the colors I choose, no matter what the current fashion.

Many weavers who spin simply make yarn without paying much attention to how the characteristics of that yarn will affect the woven fabric. Simply making yarn does work and you can end up with textiles that are both useful and beautiful. But if you take the time to understand the foundations of yarn construction, you can make fabrics that are truly exemplary. As a spinner, you get to choose what fibers, grist, twist, and colors will be put into your yarn and, therefore, exactly what your yarn will look like and how it will behave when transformed into fabric.

Consider the advantages spinners have over commercial yarn mills—we can search out specific breeds of sheep and other fiber animals, blend any combination of fibers, specify the exact size of the yarn, select the direction and amount of twist, and choose the exact color by dyeing the fiber or yarn ourselves, bypassing the commercial mills and "experts" who determine what yarns and colors will be manufactured in a given year. In short, spinners can be individualistic. We can make exactly the yarn we want in the quantities we need.

The majority of fabrics I weave are for clothing, and these are the fabrics of focus in this book—usable items that will withstand everyday wear and washing. I've also included a gallery of handspun, handwoven goods from other weavers—friends of mine with a variety of styles—that provide a glimpse of what's possible when weaving with handspun yarn.

It's important to know that there are no specifics for any type of fabric, fiber, or project. But I believe that there are some parameters. The yarn has to hold up to the process of weaving and finishing, be suitable for the end project, and, I hope, be aesthetically pleasing to the maker. The way that these goals are achieved can vary greatly from spinner to spinner and from weaver to weaver. In these pages, I will explain what I learned from my samples and how I proceeded from sample to project. In ideal cases, my process was linear—I started with a project idea or a fiber, sampled until I found how best to use the fiber for a given project, wove the fabric, and then turned that fabric into something useful.

Weavers have woven with handspun yarns for millennia. Until the advent of industrial spinning in the eighteenth century, every textile was handspun—clothing, bedding, curtains, towels, tents, sails, and rugs and carpets worldwide. With the Industrial Revolution in the nineteenth century, weaving and handspinning as an everyday task began to recede into obscurity. Today, few people understand the mechanics or complexity of how fabric is made. And somehow, many of those who have taken up handweaving as a hobby subscribe to the mistaken idea that handspun yarns are inferior to commercial yarns where weaving is concerned.

Spinning yarn for weaving is no more difficult than any other spinning. Take the time to spin and weave as often as your schedule and interest allows and make samples with your yarns. There will be times when your yarn doesn't function as well as you would like or doesn't look the way you imagined, but the more projects you spin and weave, the more successes you will have. Make lots of samples. Make lots of things. Look critically at your work. Make more. And, as if by magic, one day you will realize that you know just what yarn you want to make, how to make it, and how to weave it into the perfect cloth.

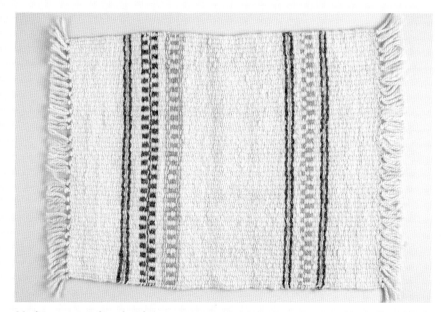

My first weaving from handspun yarns.

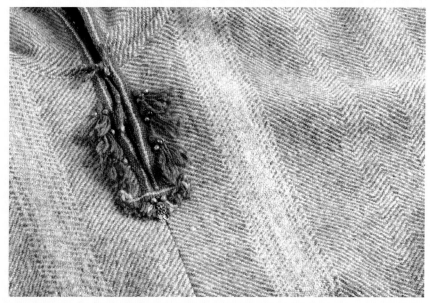

A poncho that I spun and wove in 1985 from the wool of my sheep.

FREQUENTLY ASKED Questions

I've already spun some yarn. What can I weave with it? Or how can I tell if it's suitable for weaving?

All yarn can be used for weaving, either as warp or weft. The fiber, grist, and amount of twist in your yarn will help you determine what it can be used for. For example, a heavy wool could make a nice blanket or shawl. A fine, tightly twisted alpaca could be nice for a garment. Weaving a sample before committing all of your yarn to a large project is always a good idea.

How can I tell if my handspun yarn is suitable for warp?

Yarn used as warp will be subjected to lengthwise tension and some abrasion. To test the strength, or soundness, of a yarn, pull sharply on a strand with both hands.

If the yarn snaps easily, be gentle while warping and weaving, or use it just for weft. If the yarn slowly drifts apart under this pressure, there may not be enough twist for it to hold up in a warp. Keep in mind that lengthwise tension is averaged over all of the strands in a warp. The more ends that there are across the weaving width, the less stress is applied to each one.

To test how your yarn holds up to abrasion resistance, hold a piece of the yarn under tension and run your thumbnail back and forth along it at least twenty times. If it frays, fuzzes, or pulls apart, it probably shouldn't be used as warp.

How can you bear to lose handspun yarn to loom waste (i.e., thrums)?

Loom waste is a fact of life for weavers. But, you can cut down on some of the waste by including fringe on your project. I like to save the rest of the thrums for other applications, such as embroidery, rug hooking, or knotted pile. And remember, you can always spin more yarn!

How can you bear to cut into handspun/handwoven fabric?

You can make more! Weave several pieces of fabric so that each is not so precious and solitary. Then cut one!

I don't sew. What can I weave that doesn't require sewing?

Scarves, shawls, blankets, tea towels, tablecloths, runners, and napkins, for example. If you have a friend who sews, you might be able to work out a trade for your handwoven fabrics!

How much fiber should I buy if I want to make a ...?

Buy lots! You can estimate the amount of fiber you'll need by weighing something similar out of a similar fiber—your woven winter jacket or a blanket from your bed, for example. But buy more than just that weight: your yarn may be different than that used in a similar item and there will be take-up, shrinkage, and loom waste in the weaving process.

Once you've spun a sample of yarn, you can use the warp calculations on page 25 to determine how many yards (including take-up, shrinkage, and loom waste) you'll need for a particular project.

How long does it take to spin and weave a ...?

By far, spinning accounts for most of the time in any handspun, handwoven project. While it may take days, weeks, or months to spin all the yarn needed, it may take just a few hours or days to weave it. But keep in mind that throwing the shuttle, changing sheds, and beating is exercise and you might want to break it out into several short sessions to prevent muscle fatigue.

For the kimono shown on page 106, it took twelve hours to warp the loom, weave the fabric, and sew the garment. I spent four months spinning the yarn.

What wheel(s) do you use?

For most of the projects in this book, I used a Lendrum 30" (76 cm) left-flyer Saxony wheel.

Can you weave with spindle-spun yarn?

Yes! You can also use spindle- and wheel-spun yarns in the same project (see the silk scarf on page 96). Because you make your yarn by your own hands, you can adjust the grist and twist no matter what tool you use to spin with.

How soon do I have to use my handspun yarn? Will it go "bad" at some point?

Handspun yarn is no different than commercial yarn: if properly washed and stored, the skeins should last indefinitely. If an older yarn feels stiff, it may contain residual spinning oils or lanolin and should be washed carefully in hot water and detergent to remove them.

What loom(s) do you use?

For most of the projects in this book, I used a 32" (81.5 cm) eight-shaft Gilmore jack-type floor loom.

What kind of loom should I buy?

You should buy a loom that fits your needs. Looms are like other tools: they should suit the purpose and fit the maker ergonomically. Think about the type of weaving you would like to do—blankets, rugs, scarves, or fabric—and choose a loom that's geared for that type of project. Also, find a loom that fits your body type. There are looms that are more comfortable for short or tall weavers and those who have long arms and legs. If possible, try out a few looms before you invest in one that might not work for you.

CHAPTER ONE
handspun samples
AND *fabric*

HANDSPINNERS WHO WEAVE TODAY have absolute control over the fabrics they make. We live in a global economy with access to fibers from all over the world, and more fibers are available to any one spinner than at any time in history. We can find wools from a wide variety of breeds of sheep, and hair and down from goats, camelids, bison, yaks, musk ox, dogs, cats, and rabbits. We have silk fiber from pure white domesticated *Bombyx mori* and any number of wild silks. We can find cottons in many lengths and natural colors; bast fibers such as flax, hemp, and ramie; and even spin regenerated cellulose or synthetic fibers, if we choose. We decide how to spin these fibers, whether to ply them, dye them, or use them in their natural color. We can follow a tradition from our geographic region or heritage, or be influenced by far-off cultures. We can make textiles of all kinds: blankets, rugs, bands, bags, yardage, and household goods.

Over the years that I have been a spinner, I have taken lots of classes and listened to lots of advice. Some information has been helpful, even crucial to my understanding and ability to make yarn and fabric. But some information either did not apply or was contradicted by the work that I did. Weaving is a huge and varied field, and not all rules will apply to all fibers, fabrics, or situations. I decided to test some oft-repeated truisms to see if they made a difference in my fabric or did not apply.

Which fibers shrink most? Felt more? Fuzz (fibrillate) more in finishing? How does twist affect the structure and surface of the fabric? How many ways can I blend colors as a spinner? How does varied grist in the same fiber change the hand, drape, weight, and utility of a fabric?

FACTORS THAT AFFECT FABRIC HAND, or How the Fabric Feels

As a spinner and weaver, you can make an infinite number of fabrics through the following variables:

✖ fiber choice—from soft fine fibers to long coarse ones

✖ spinning technique

✖ yarn diameter, or thickness

✖ number of plies in the yarn

✖ amount of twist in the singles and plies

✖ sett—the number of warp ends per inch of cloth (abbreviated epi)

✖ weft choice

✖ weave structure

✖ beat—the number of weft picks per inch of cloth (abbreviated ppi)

✖ finishing methods

It was very freeing for me to spin for samples: they are quick, require very little investment in fiber and time, and taught me a lot—even the samples in which not much happened. Some oft-repeated truisms were confirmed, others, not.

If we truly put hands to tools, we learn things in a way no teacher can teach. And from all this busy-ness I learned a few things. Perhaps what I learned is only true for me, my way of working, or only one fabric, but I'm fine with that. I can speak clearly and confidently about what happened with my fiber, my yarn, my fabrics.

In addition, I got a lot of ideas. I have more to do now than ever, which, good or bad, seems always the case: work generates work. There is just no substitute for doing the work. No talking about it, no wishing or thinking about it, no reading about it, no journaling about what I will do next, no daydreaming or imagining how things would work, no repeating truisms will teach what the fibers really have to say: nothing beats just getting things done.

getting started

Before you can weave fabric, you need to spin yarn for the warp and/or weft. Before you can spin yarn, you need to choose a fiber or a group of fibers and prepare them for spinning. The fabric you want in the end will determine some of these choices—a warm wool for a jacket, a fine silk for a shawl. Look around your house for successful garments or household fabric and take cues from the fibers used, the weights of the fabric, and how the fabric is woven.

Pygora fabric with singles and plied yarn.

FIBER CHOICE

For the fabrics presented in this book, I limited my selections to natural fibers—a renewable resource available in some form on every continent. These are the fibers with which I am most familiar and the ones that have proven successful in a variety of garment fabrics. I further limited my selections to fibers that have been commercially prepared and are widely available through retail and mail-order sources. There are a number of ways that fiber can be prepared—top or roving, carded in batts, or simply bundles of raw fibers—and each imparts different characteristics in the yarn. I limited myself to two basic types of protein fiber preparations—top or roving in wool, alpaca, pygora, mohair, silk, and blends of these protein fibers (see Resources on page 134).

WOOL is a protein fiber that comes from sheep. Depending on the breed, it can range from fine to coarse and from short to long fibers, with the crimp ranging from tight to loose. Wool is used for a wide array of fabrics for clothing and household textiles. It is one of the first fibers I learned to spin and it remains a favorite for warmth, comfort, durability, and its ability to take dye. It is easy to process from the animal to the finished product. Because wool has so many attractive qualities, it is often blended with other fibers.

The varieties of wools available are seemingly endless, with breeds and crossbreeds developed for every purpose from soft, fine clothing to durable rugs and upholstery. However, the sheep breed alone does not guarantee particular qualities, as there can be considerable variation from one fleece to another, even within the same breed.

silk/Merino

mohair

You can use two different fibers to emphasize the fabric design. In this sample, a mohair warp yarn (left) is combined with a silk/Merino (one ply of each) weft (right). The shine in the silk emphasizes the twill structure in the fabric. Spun and woven by Amy Norris.

It is therefore important to spin and sample each batch of the fiber as the first step in planning any fabric.

FINE WOOLS, such as Merino, Polwarth, and Cormo, are typically used for fabrics that are intended to be worn next to the skin or over a single light under-layer. Being at the finer end of the diameter spectrum for wool, they feel soft to the touch. Fine fibers such as these are also commonly blended with silk, which adds durability and luster without compromising the inherent softness.

MEDIUM WOOLS, such as Bluefaced Leicester (BFL), Shetland, and Corriedale, make wonderful warm mid-weight garments. Because they have larger fiber diameters, they are slightly sturdier and more resistant to abrasion. These wools are commonly used for sweaters, vests, and lightweight jackets.

LONGWOOLS, such as Romney, Lincoln, Coopworth, Wensleydale, and Masham, are strong and durable. Yet larger in diameter, these fibers are quite resistant to abrasion and typically have longer staple lengths. They are best for sturdy outerwear, rugs, bands, and bags.

MOHAIR, the fiber from Angora goats, is also a protein fiber. It takes dye well and adds drape, shine, and strength to fabrics. It is often blended with wool to add luster, durability, and depth of color to the spun yarn. Mohair comes in a range of fiber diameters from very fine—usually kid mohair, which is considered wearable—to durable, rug-quality coarse fibers from adult goats.

PYGORA results from a cross between Angora goats and pygmy goats. It can range from very fine to quite coarse, depending on the grade, which varies from animal to animal and from year to year. It is labeled at the point of

Different fibers behave differently in the same fabric, as illustrated by the Merino and Bluefaced Leicester stripes in the warp of these samples (left: unwashed; right: washed).

purchase as A (top quality), B, or C (lowest quality). The finer grades of pygora add durability and shine to wool blends, as well as a soft halo on the surface of the fabric. Spun alone, it can be lustrous and extremely soft.

CASHMERE, one of the finest fibers, comes from the short, fluffy down coat of cashmere goats. Although cashmere goats produce a range of fiber fineness, only the fibers that meet specific standards can be labeled cashmere. Cashmere is used alone or it can be blended with wool, silk, or other fibers for fine clothing.

ALPACA is a protein fiber from the camelid group, which includes camels, llamas, alpacas, and vicuñas. The fiber is generally warmer than an equal weight of wool or mohair, has nice drape in fabric, is durable, and takes dye beautifully. But it has very little elasticity and will stretch if not held in by a fabric construction that supports the weight. Alpaca is ideal for weaving because the warp supports

the weft and gives stability to the fabric. Just like wools, the quality of alpaca fiber can vary from animal to animal. Yarns that blend alpaca with wool can have more elasticity and recovery, which is the ability to return to shape once wrinkled or stretched.

SILK, another protein fiber, comes from the cocoons produced by silk worms. Cultivated silk (*Bombyx mori*) is bright white, while wild silks—such as tussah, muga, and eri—are various shades of off-white to golden beige. The best silk fiber is reeled, not spun, but the reeling process only uses part of each cocoon—the rest can be cleaned and prepared for commercial spinning. It is this leftover fiber that is available to handspinners as top or bricks. Silk can be spun alone or used in blends to add luster, strength, and durability to other fibers. The very shortest fibers remaining from the silk reeling and spinning processes are carded to be spun into a rough yarn

Fabric from wool spun from top (left) has a smooth surface; fabric from wool spun from roving (right) has a fuzzier surface.

called "noil." Silk noil retains some of the strength, durability, and drape without the luster. It can be useful on its own or added to other fibers in blends. I use it mostly as weft.

I am convinced that the success of any project is largely determined by the careful choice of a suitable fiber. A fine wool will never make a longwearing carpet, no matter how much twist or how many plies the yarn may have. And a coarse wool will never be soft enough for next-to-the-skin wear, no matter how soft and fluffy the yarn is spun. The fiber will always assert its general character in the finished project.

FIBER PREPARATION

I like to use well-prepared fibers, but I don't often prepare much fiber myself. If I buy a fleece, I send it to a small mill where it is carded into roving. I also like to buy fibers that are already prepared into top (in which uniform-length fibers are aligned parallel to each other) or roving (in which the fibers vary more in staple length and are less aligned in the preparation). Top is a dense preparation; roving is loose and airy. I dye some of my own fibers, but I also like to purchase ones that have already been dyed (see Resources). Much of this is personal—I'm not very good at fiber preparation (it's never been a priority), and I prefer to spend my time spinning and weaving.

MAKING Samples

A sample can save you from a failed project or from hours of unnecessary spinning and weaving, and is well worth the effort. Handspun yarn is not inherently better than commercial yarn, but it certainly can be. As spinners who weave, we can make yarn that is exceptionally suited to the project at hand.

When I started spinning and weaving thirty-five years ago, I didn't have access to much information so I wove samples to experiment with the fibers that were available—a practice that I highly recommend. Through samples and using the projects that you do weave, you will learn more about spinning yarn for weaving than any information I can present here.

Most of my fabrics begin with two-ply handspun wool, silk, alpaca, or mohair in a variety of grists that is washed and dried before it is woven. I typically use a close sett for warp-dominant fabrics. However, for the purposes of this book, I spun and wove a few samples that deviated from my norm to test some theories and to see if I could improve my fabrics. I tried spinning with more or less twist, changing twist direction, not washing the yarn before weaving, using singles for warp, and I tried different setts.

In addition to providing useful information on twist direction, twist amount, yarn finishing choices, weft choice, shrinkage, and fabric finishing preferences, such samples will help you accurately calculate how much finished yarn you'll need for a project. Along with knowing the length and width of finished fabric you'll need for a particular project, being able to estimate the amount of take-up, draw-in, and shrinkage will help you spin the right amount of yarn (allowing some extra for good measure). Weaving is much more enjoyable when you're certain you'll end up with enough fabric for your intended project.

For the samples and projects in this book, I have used commercially prepared top, bricks, or roving. Except for re-carding some of the fibers together in small batches for color variations, I always began with prepared fibers.

The way that the fiber is prepared can have a subtle effect on the look and feel of the spun yarn. For illustration, I spun yarn for two medium-grade wool fabrics, shown in the photo on page 20. The yarn for one is spun from roving (a process that opens and begins to align the fibers for spinning); the other is spun from top (a process that sorts out short fibers and aligns the fibers more thoroughly). All things being equal—spinning method, yarn size, sett, and weave structure—roving (right) produces fabric with a fuzzier surface than top (left), which produces fabric that appears quite smooth. What does this tell us? For a warmer wool fabric—one that traps air and retains loft—you'll get a loftier yarn if you spin roving than if you spin prepared top. But don't be mistaken. Both will make beautiful wool fabrics; they will just be different.

When choosing fibers, my advice is to buy the best fibers you can. Whether you prepare the fiber yourself or buy prepared fiber from individuals, mills, or shops, take care to choose the best quality you can afford. Keep in mind that "best" is defined differently by different people—the best quality (whether the cleanest, the longest, the finest, or the best prepared), the most local and sustainable, the least environmentally damaging, etc. Whatever ruler you use to measure "best," use it. While it is possible to make a mess out of good fibers, it takes very hard work to turn bad fibers into a beautiful product.

COMBINING FIBERS

When choosing fiber for a project, keep in mind that fiber from different sources can behave differently when woven into fabric and these differences can lead to differential shrinkage, in which the surface of the fabric becomes irregular and undulating. This can be an unwelcome surprise if your intention was uniform fabric. The best way to avoid differential shrinkage is to use fiber of a single type—coarse, medium, or fine wool; the same grade of pygora or silk—or blend the fibers into the same preparation.

Differential shrinkage between the grouped ends of the Corriedale and Lincoln–Corriedale cross caused a seersucker effect in this fabric.

Fiber from a variety of alpaca fleeces are combined for color variation in this shawl.
To avoid possible differential shrinkage, I alternated single ends of the different colors.

But there will be times when you will want to include fibers from different sources. Maybe you'll want to combine several colors of natural fibers from the same breed, not all of which are produced by the same animal. Or you might want to combine wool in your stash that has no source identification. Or, perhaps you've spun a number of small bits of similar yarn over time that you'd like to combine in the same project.

If you want to minimize the effects of differential shrinkage, alternate single ends or small groups of the same yarn in regular fashion throughout the warp. This creates uniformity across the width of the fabric and the various yarns will work together to balance out the overall shrinkage, as in the alpaca fabric shown above as well as the fabrics shown on page 24. But you can use differential shrinkage to your advantage by grouping the various yarns in the warp to create beautifully undulating surfaces, as in

the fabric shown on page 25. In both of these samples, the Merino has shrunk more than the silk or Bluefaced Leicester.

It's important to know about the possibility of differential shrinkage and plan for it, rather than be surprised when your fabric doesn't turn out the way you envisioned. This is where samples can be invaluable. Even if you've already warped your loom, you can weave a sample in the first few inches, cut the sample from the loom, and then wash and finish it as you plan to finish your fabric to determine how the yarns will work together. If there is differential shrinkage, you might be able to re-sley the yarns or replace the worst offenders with something less troublesome without having to abandon the warp altogether.

This fabric was made from similar wools of unknown origins.

For this shawl, I combined cashmere from different sources that I spun over a period of years and that I never intended to use in the same project.

Grouped ends of Blueface Leicester and Merino create a smooth fabric on the loom (left) and a seersucker effect after washing (right).

Grouped warp ends of Merino and silk will also create puckers as the wool shrinks with washing. Samples spun and woven by Amy Norris.

WARP Calculations

For the final width and length of fabric you need, multiply the width of the warp in the reed by the number of ends per inch by the length of the warp on the loom. You will also need to add the estimated amount of take-up, draw-in, shrinkage, and loom waste.

For example, for a finished fabric measuring 15" (38 cm) wide and 4 yd (3.6 m) long woven from two-ply yarn that measures 18 wraps per inch (wpi), I will plan a sett of 15 ends per inch (epi).

I will typically plan for about 10% widthwise draw-in due to the interlacement of the weft with the warp, and about 3% shrinkage due to washing and fulling, for a total widthwise loss of 13%.

I will also plan for about 4% take-up due to the interlacement of the weft with the warp, and 8% shrinkage, for a total loss of 12%, plus 1 yd (0.9 m) loss due to loom waste.

To get a finished width of 15" (38 cm), my weaving width will be:

15" (38 cm) finished width + 13% draw-in and shrinkage = 16.95", which I round up to 17" (43 cm)

To get a finished length of 4 yd (3.6 m), my total warp length will be:

4 yd (3.6 m) finished length + 12% (17.3" or 44 cm) take-up and shrinkage plus 1 yd (0.9 m) loom waste = 5.5 yd (5 m) total

To calculate the number of individual warp ends, I'll multiply:

17" (43 cm) width in reed × 15 epi = 255 warp ends total

To calculate the total number of yards of warp needed, I'll multiply:

255 warp ends total × 5.5 total yd (5 m) = 1,402 yd (1,275 m)

This gives me the minimum amount of warp yarn to spin. But I always spin extra for sampling at the beginning of a warp, and to test the method of finishing, if needed.

spinning

As spinners, we have unlimited control over four primary aspects of yarn construction: 1) the type of fiber (or fibers) used—we can select a fiber or blend of fibers to suit any project; 2) the amount of twist that's put into the yarn—we can control how much the fiber is twisted and the direction in which it is twisted as it is spun; 3) the size of the singles—we can spin very thick to very thin yarn, depending on our purpose; and 4) the optimum number of strands to ply together for the project at hand. In addition, we can dye the fleece, roving, or yarn any color we wish without being limited to the colors that are currently in vogue and commercially available. Put all these variables together, and we spinners have infinite yarns at our disposal.

SPINNING WHEELS

I own three spinning wheels. My primary wheel is a left-flyer Lendrum Saxony with a 30" (76 cm) wheel that can be set up as a double-drive mechanism or scotch tension (flyer lead) with a brake on the bobbin. Most of the yarns for the projects in this book were spun on this wheel, set up for scotch tension.

I also own an upright folding wheel (for spinning while away from home) with scotch tension and an electric spinner, which is also set up with scotch tension. I used the electric spinner mostly to ply yarns. In addition, I spun and plied some of the yarns for this book on spindles.

The most important thing I learned while spinning so many projects over a short period of time is that the drive band should be replaced often, and the wheel should be oiled regularly. The drive band on my Saxony is a softly spun multiple-ply cotton twine. The band stretches a bit with each spinning session and eventually loses it elasticity, becomes so smooth that it slips rather than turns the wheel, or becomes too long for adjusting the tension. My folding wheel uses an elastic drive band that stretches over time. I'm in the habit of always having spare drive bands on hand.

My wheels, bobbins, and whorls are neither special nor unique—they are all commercially available. Other than setting both of my wheels to operate with scotch tension for consistency, I did not use any special tools or settings. The miles and miles of consistent yarn needed to weave fabrics is up to the skill of the spinner, not the unique qualities of the tools.

I am a firm believer that it's best to acquire just a few quality tools and to learn how to operate those tools well. If you're familiar with your wheel, understand how it works, and know how it feels when it's working properly, you'll know right away when something is amiss. I sit down at the same wheel nearly every day, and I can instantly feel when it's not working properly. It takes only moments to change drive bands or adjust the drive band tension, oil the wheel, check that the yarn has a clear path onto the bobbin, and fine-tune the tension and alignments as necessary. As a daily spinner, I know exactly how my tools behave and how to correct any anomalies. It would be much more difficult to maintain consistent yarn if I jumped from wheel to wheel.

It takes long hours over weeks and sometimes over months to spin for a project. Therefore, you want to find

SPINNING FROM THE END

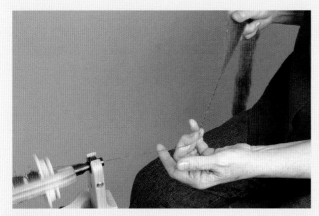

Roving or top can be drafted directly from the end of the preparation.

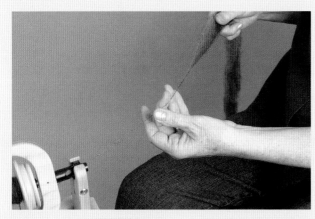

Hold the fiber loosely and position your hands further apart than the staple length of the fiber.

Watch the drafting triangle to make sure that the fibers are primarily aligned as they enter the twist zone and that the fiber amount remains consistent.

SPINNING OVER THE FOLD

Roving or top can be drafted from the side of the preparation by holding a bundle over the index finger of your drafting hand.

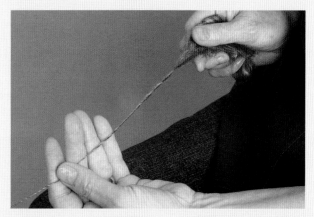

As the fiber bundle over your finger diminishes, hold the fiber loosely in your drafting hand, still drafting from the fold.

a comfortable spinning chair, a spinning wheel or spindle, and a comfortable series of working positions so you can spin comfortably and without strain. In general, the act of spinning should be relaxing.

SPINNING TECHNIQUE

I generally spin one of two ways: point of contact long draw (the fibers are drawn into the drafting triangle by the twist) and double draft long draw (the fibers are drafted ahead of the twist and attenuated to stabilization as twist is inserted). I most often spin from the end of the top or roving but will spin "over the fold" when using slick fibers such as silk. Whichever way I spin, I watch the drafting triangle to make sure the fibers feed mostly aligned into the twist. For the most part, I spin fine yarns with lots of twist and I am more concerned about maintaining even grist than I am about how the fibers are prepared or held as I spin. I have successfully spun wool from both roving and top this way (see the samples of two wool fabrics on page 20), as well as silk, alpaca, mohair, and pygora.

FIBER ALIGNMENT

The number of fibers and their orientation as they enter the drafting triangle determines the character of the yarn you will work with. Fibers are either more or less aligned as they enter the twist zone, and the length of time they are held as twist is inserted helps determine the hand of the yarn. The fibers also are under tension as the twist enters the drafting zone—either by the pull of the entering twist itself or because I am pulling back on the fibers. They are neither slack nor disorganized in the drafting triangle, rather, they are taut and enter primarily straight on. This makes for a smoother and more abrasion-resistant yarn.

For consistent fiber alignment in handspun yarn, I use commercially prepared top and spin point-of-contact, allowing the twist to pull new fibers into the drafting triangle and being careful to impart sufficient twist into the fiber before it passes through the orifice. Less alignment occurs if you spin off the fold (the fibers are drafted from the edge of the fiber preparation). The amount of twist inserted determines whether the yarn is firm or lofty.

Sometimes spinners take great pains to make sure that all the fibers in their yarns and all the singles in each ply are spun in the same direction. You can carefully spin locks

Fibers enter the twist zone in relative alignment when spinning from prepared top.

Fibers enter the twist zone in less alignment when spinning from roving.

from butt to tip and painstakingly reorient the spun yarns before plying. All this work gets jumbled in the weaving process, however, as warp yarns are run back and forth when measured on a warping board or warping reel and weft yarns cross back and forth across the web. You can keep the fiber oriented in a single direction through sectional warping, but the orientation of the fibers in the weft will always crisscross the warp as the fabric is woven.

TWIST

Without twist, the fibers wouldn't hold together to form yarn. The amount of twist and number of plies needed for a weaving yarn varies, depending on how it's going to be used. Fabrics can be woven from singles or plied yarns in either or both warp and weft, or in any combination.

For fabrics, my favorite yarn for warp has a tight twist and consists of at least two plies for strength and durability. Yarns with substantial twist will resist pilling in use as well as stand up to the rigors of the weaving and finishing processes. For especially sturdy textiles such as rugs, bags, and tablet weavings, I impart an even firmer twist and ply more than two strands together. Weft yarns, which aren't held under tension and aren't subject to abrasion in the reed or as much tension in the weaving process, can be lightly twisted and either singles or plied.

Keep in mind that tightly twisted yarns do not necessarily produce dense, stiff fabrics. It is the fiber that you begin with and the grist to which you spin it that will most directly determine the drape, hand, and feel of a fabric. Fine protein fibers, even when spun with a firm twist, can retain their soft hand and weave into soft fabrics. Sturdy fibers will make more durable fabrics when spun firmly to enhance their longwearing characteristics.

Yarn can be twisted clockwise (called the Z direction) and counterclockwise (called the S direction). Both directions are equally valid and you might like to try both to see if you have a preference. Most fabrics are made from yarns that are all spun in the same direction, but you can get some interesting special effects if you mix yarns with different twist directions (see the sidebar on page 30).

Many weavers choose soft and fluffy yarns for their wefts. But soft yarns often don't hold up to the stresses of tension, abrasion, and finishing necessary in weaving so I tend to shy away from them. This doesn't mean that I can't get a soft hand in my fabrics—fine fibers, even when tightly spun, will fibrillate to create a halo on the surface of the yarn or fabric during the weaving and finishing process, resulting in a soft hand.

Sized (left) and unsized (right) samples of soft-twist two-ply mohair at 16 wpi, sett at 15 epi, and lightly brushed.

To compare fabrics woven with firmly and softly twisted yarn, I spun a softly twisted two-ply kid mohair for warp and weft. The yarn measures 16 wraps per inch (wpi) and was sett at 15 epi for a width of 10" (25.5 cm). As I wove, the yarns drifted apart, stretched out of shape, pulled loose, and made for an unpleasant weaving experience.

I decided to set up a second warp with the same yarn and sett, but this time I sized the yarns by dipping them in gelatin and allowing them to dry before I warped the loom. Surprisingly, there was no improvement in how they wove—the warps drifted apart and fiber kept sliding out of the low-twist yarn.

I finished both samples, leaving evidence of repaired warps, and lightly brushed them in the pressing process. In the end, the fabrics weren't any softer than the firmly twisted kid mohair used on page 61, and they were unstable and annoying to work with.

The lesson here is that the soft hand in fabric comes from the fiber used in the yarn, not the amount of twist. Spin with enough twist in your yarns to hold your yarns together for whatever construction techniques your fabric requires. You can then finish the fabric in a way that will enhance the fiber characteristics.

TWIST Direction

How do twist amount and twist direction affect the fabric? Does the weave structure matter? Does a change in twist direction change the surface of a fabric?

To evaluate opposing twist, I spun some yarns clockwise in the "Z" direction and others counterclockwise in the "S" direction. Two Z-twist singles plied in the S direction are designated as z2s; two S-twist singles plied in the Z direction are designated as s2z.

Many years ago, I wove a bag from two-ply rayon yarn that I spun with opposing twist—some of the yarn was s2z, some was z2s. I sett the warp closely, hoping that the opposing twist in the yarns would produce a damask-like effect in the fabric. As it turned out, there was very little visual effect and the opposing twist was only noticeable in the fringe that extended beyond the bag.

I decided to explore the effects more systematically for the following samples. Using Romney top, I spun several bobbins in my usual manner: Z-twist singles plied in the S direction (z2s). Then I spun several bobbins in the opposite way—S-twist singles plied in the Z direction (s2z).

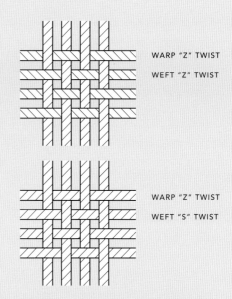

WARP "Z" TWIST
WEFT "Z" TWIST

WARP "Z" TWIST
WEFT "S" TWIST

Weft spun in the opposite direction of the warp tends to pack in closer when woven.

I have become so accustomed to spinning in the Z direction that I felt very awkward spinning in the opposite direction. Apparently, my hands and fingers have developed subtle movements that assist in my spinning in the Z direction.

For the first sample, I used weft spun in the same direction. For the others, I used weft that was spun in the opposite direction (s2z). Although I did my best to spin yarn of similar grist and tried to maintain an even beat, the samples woven with weft spun in the opposite direction tended to beat in tighter. The twist direction likely allows the weft to slide into place more closely, as shown in the illustrations at upper right. This is useful information for rug weavers, tapestry weavers, and anyone trying to make a firm fabric or one with close-packed wefts.

For the next few samples, I varied the sett and twist direction in several ways. There is very little evidence of twist variation in the appearance or hand of the five samples.

Other than the fringe, there is no apparent effect of the opposing twist in the rayon yarn used for this woven bag.

The same z2s warp was used in both of these plain-weave samples. Left: z2s weft at 11 picks per inch (ppi). Right: s2z weft at 13 ppi.

The same z2s warp and z2s weft was used in both of these twill samples. Left: twill direction from left to right. Right: twill direction from right to left.

The same z2s warp and s2z weft was used in both of these twill samples. The twill direction in the left sample is from left to right; the twill direction in the right sample is from right to left. There is little difference between the two fabrics when viewed from the front.

When the back of one fabric is viewed next to the front of the other, there seems to be more discernable difference between the two twill surfaces, but it's a subtle effect.

Romney plain weave z2s warp sett at 15 epi: z2s weft (left) and s2z weft (right).

Romney plain weave z2s warp sett at 20 epi: z2s weft (left) and s2z weft (right).

Tightly twisted Romney sett at 40 epi (left) and 30 epi (right).

Twist direction warp stripes: 15 epi (left) and 12 epi (right).

Yarns can be spun at different times with different tools and still have matching twist amounts if you pay attention and strive for consistency. The fabric shown here includes both wheel- and spindle-spun yarns. Some yarns were plied from two separate bobbins and some were plied from two ends of the same ball. All blended and wove into a cohesive fabric without noticeable variation.

Although the plain-weave samples exhibit plenty of tracking (the appearance of twill lines after washing as a result of twist energy), the tracking doesn't follow the twist direction lines—it appears totally random. In the twill samples, the twill direction line is more prominent in some combinations as light shifts across the surface of the fabric, but I don't think there is enough variation to merit the effort of spinning opposite yarns.

Finally, I examined a friend's Peruvian textile that demonstrated twist directional variation in the warp—it was tightly spun two-ply wool sett closely in a warp-faced weave. Using a very tight twist in the yarns brought out the surface variation I was looking for.

It is clear that twist amount, as well as direction and a close sett, help give this sample its surface appearance.

I also decided to try adding color to the mix. I spun a dark and a light singles in both directions, then plied them for z2s and s2z yarns. I threaded the two yarns in stripes across the warp and used an all-white weft. This sample shows interesting potential—the color change in the singles emphasizes the twist direction and the plain-weave sample has twill characteristics. I spun the yarn for this sample on spindles while traveling, and I wove it on a small handheld sample loom. I believe this effect is worth exploring with close-value color changes or widely divergent color changes. It could produce a very interesting fabric.

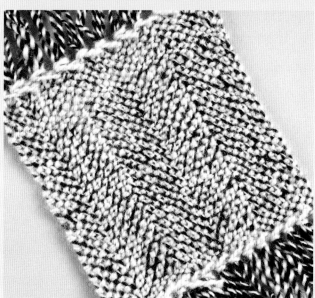

The different twist directions are emphasized when different colors are used.

Twist Angle or How Much Twist Do I Use?

Yarns intended for weaving must be able to withstand the warping, weaving, and finishing processes. The yarns are held under tension, undergo abrasion and beating during weaving, and are subject to the rigors of washing, fulling, nap raising and cropping, and, at times, tentering (drying under tension). That's a lot to ask of any yarn, handspun or otherwise. But all of this doesn't mean that fabric woven from handspun yarn can't be luxuriously soft.

It's important to understand that soft fabrics are not necessarily made from yarns that are softly twisted. Soft-twist yarns are more likely to break down and stretch during weaving and finishing than those that are firmly twisted. As long as you begin with a soft fiber, you can give it a firm twist to give it resilience and durability during the weaving and finishing processes, and the fabric you end up with will have the characteristics of that soft fiber.

There are a number of ways to quantify the amount of twist you put into your yarns—you can determine a drafting length and count treadles to develop a steady rhythm, for example, or you can measure twist angle against a chart. I've learned to spin by the look and feel of the emerging yarn, not by counting treadles or measuring twist angle. I rely on feeling the firmness of the developing yarn under my fingers to determine when there is enough and consistent twist. My singles have less twist than my plied yarns. I can easily see the angle of twist while plying, which often isn't the case when spinning the singles. Tight twist in the plying ensures that the yarns are durable enough for close-sett weaving. If you look closely at the photos of yarns in this book, you can see the amount of twist in most of the yarns.

Pull a length of yarn off the bobbin and let it twist back on itself to observe the twist angle.

Varying amounts of twist in the weft yarns caused puckers in this wool fabric.

To maintain consistent spin angle throughout the yarn for a particular project, spin a sample and keep it attached to a card by your wheel. Stop often to compare your work with the sample. Pull a length of yarn off the bobbin behind the orifice (yarn that hasn't passed the orifice does not have the same amount of twist as the yarn that has accumulated on the bobbin), and let it fold back on itself to observe the twist angle periodically as you spin.

After you've settled into a rhythm of spinning, you will be able to feel for consistency instead of counting your treadles or stopping repeatedly to check the twist angle. Keep in mind that it can take weeks or months to spin sufficient yarn for a project and that you'll want to be as consistent as possible throughout. Therefore, every time you return to your wheel, take time to compare your yarn to your sample to make sure you don't deviate from your intentions.

Be aware that inconsistent twist in the yarn can cause puckers in woven fabric. To mitigate this variation, alternate yarns in the warp end by end and in the weft pick by pick, or limit the yarns to narrow sections—less than an inch (2.5 cm) wide—or alternate two or more yarns in the warp and weft, much as if you were using a mixed warp.

In general, loft and elasticity—produced by light twist—are not qualities you want in weaving yarns. But that doesn't mean you can't have lofty, elastic fabrics. Depending on your choice of fibers, how those fibers are prepared, how much twist is inserted as they are spun, the structure in which they are woven, and the way the cloth is finished, you'll get all the loft and elasticity you'll want.

The best-quality fine wools, such as Cormo and Merino, or fine hair fibers, such as kid mohair and alpaca, can be showcased in weaving. Their fine fibers are captured by twist and by the weave structure, but will bloom in the finishing process to reflect their inherent softness.

Regardless of how the fibers are prepared, watch the drafting triangle as you spin to control the alignment and amount of fiber that is twisted.

Alternate yarns in the warp and weft to minimize the overall effect of twist variations. In this sample, I alternated the warp and weft yarns end by end and pick by pick.

Use yarns in narrow sections to control the effect of any one yarn in the fabric. The warp yarns in these three samples have different amounts of twist. The varied amount of twist shows up in the sample (left) with a fine weft; the heavier weft obscures the twist variation in the warp in the twill and plain-weave samples (center and right).

JOINING FIBER TO FIBER

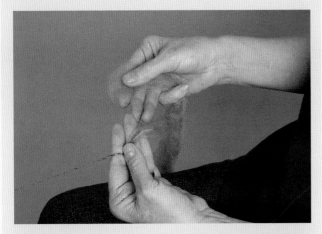

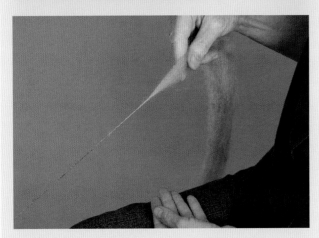

For the best results, join fiber to fiber. Splay the ends of the old and new fibers (top). Overlap the splayed ends as you spin (center). The fibers form a strong join (bottom).

JOINING FIBER TO YARN

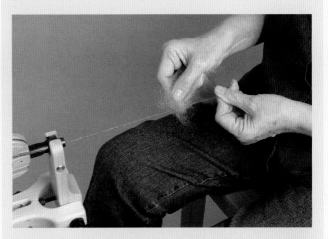

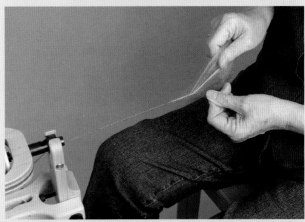

To join fiber to yarn, catch the splayed ends of the fiber on fibers that have already been twisted into yarn (top), allow the twist to travel into the new fiber (center), and continue spinning the new fiber (bottom).

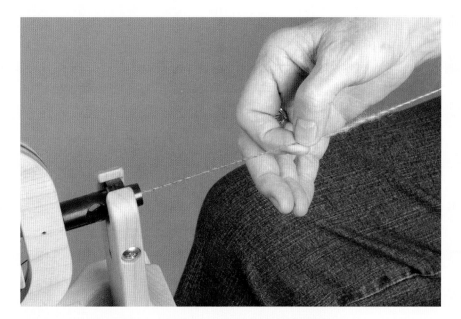

I generally hold my hands loosely and draft open-handed to help ensure the fibers are aligned as they enter the drafting triangle.

JOINING FIBER

There will be times when you'll need to join a new source of fiber to the yarn you're spinning. When doing so, you'll want to make these joins as invisible and as strong as possible for yarns that will be used for warp. Joins are most secure when fiber is added to fiber because the ends catch the new fiber and blend them into the existing yarn. Joins made by wrapping the new fiber around existing yarns can unwrap under the abrasion that occurs with weaving, unless these joins are further secured in plied yarns.

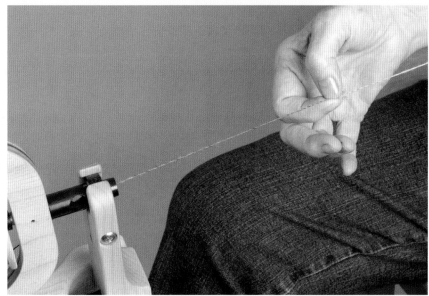

A fiber-to-yarn join may not be very stable and can drift apart when abraded. Therefore, yarns with this type of join are less stable when used as singles in warps.

PLYING

Spinning necessarily adds twist to fibers as singles are created. No matter how the twist might be tamed so that the yarns can be used for weaving, it can reactivate during the finishing process to create its own surface texture in a woven fabric. Twist reactivation can be quite helpful if you want a yarn that traps air for insulating fabrics such as jackets and blankets. The twist that you put into a singles will remain in the fabric woven with those singles. Plain-weave fabrics woven from singles yarns have the potential to produce irregular surface textures as the twist reactivates during finishing.

However, when two or more singles are plied, the original twist angle, which is worked in one direction, will be opposed by the direction of plying, which is worked in the opposite direction. As a result, the fibers end up aligned lengthwise in the yarn.

The active twist in singles can be tempered somewhat when two or more strands are plied together. The less active twist makes plied yarns easier to work with and can eliminate some finishing steps before the yarn is ready to use for weaving. For example, blocking may not be necessary. While weave structure and amount of twist are always factors, fabrics woven from plied yarns can look smooth and crisp. I usually ply two strands together when I spin yarn for weaving, no matter what fiber I use. But there are good reasons to ply three or more strands, especially when you want exceptionally sturdy and smooth-surfaced yarns for rug warps, band weaving, card weaving, or bags, or when you want to blend colors together (see photo at right).

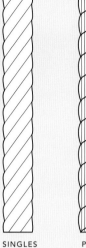 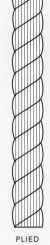

SINGLES   PLIED

In a singles, all the fibers are twisted in one direction. In plied yarns, the fibers are twisted both in the direction of the singles and in the direction of the ply, and end up about parallel. This is what mitigated the twist energy in the samples shown on pages 30, 31, and 32.

z   s

I spun singles from five different colors of silk, then blended them in three-ply yarns to create the subtle color blending in this silk scarf.

Three-ply yarns result in very sturdy fabrics.

GRIST OR THICKNESS

You have full control over the grist, or size, of the yarn you spin, from very thick alpaca singles for a shawl to very fine plied wool for fabric to tailor. In general, the end product will dictate the size of the yarn you'll want to spin. Grist of yarn is usually calculated as the length per unit of weight and is reported as yards or meters per pound. Another approach is to count the number of wraps per inch (wpi) for the purposes of determining sett and consistency.

Wrap yarn around an inch gauge or ruler for 1" (2.5 cm) to determine the number of wraps per inch (wpi).

Yarns spun for clothing can vary widely in grist, depending on the weight of the garment desired. The same medium-grade wool was used in both of these fabrics: on the left, the yarn measured 24 wpi and was sett at 20 epi; on the right, the yarn measured 12 wpi and was sett at 15 epi.

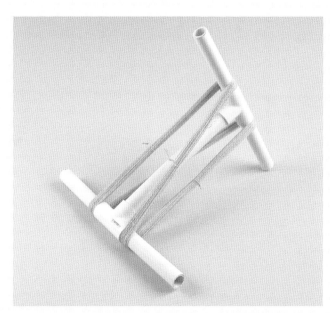

For a firmly twisted yarn, I wind wet yarn on a PVC niddy-noddy, then wash it and leave it to dry under tension.

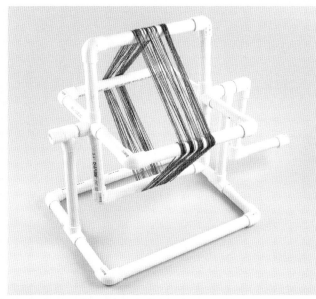

For a little tension without stretching, I wrap the wet yarn around a PVC yarn blocker.

To measure wpi, wrap the yarn under little tension around a ruler or inch gauge and count the number of strands that are in one inch (2.5 cm) of width.

Scarves and shawls can be woven from almost any size of yarn. As long as the finished piece drapes or wraps around the wearer nicely, it can range from extremely light and diaphanous to thick and blanket-like. On the other hand, many of the fabrics for this book were intended to be cut and sewn into garments. To prevent the fabrics from being too bulky, especially along seams, most are woven with relatively fine yarns that measure between 15 and 18 wpi, and some are even finer.

FINISHING THE YARN

Before I weave with handspun, I generally wind the yarn into a skein, wash it with a mild detergent or scouring agent suitable for wool, and allow it to airdry thoroughly (usually not under tension unless the yarn is especially tightly twisted, such as rug warp). I've also been known to wind a warp fresh off the bobbins, then wash the yarn as a warp chain before I begin weaving if the yarn does not need to be dried under tension. Washing the yarn stabilizes the twist, pre-shrinks it, and helps distribute any variations in twist along the length, all of which ensures a more consistent woven fabric. It also makes the yarn easier to handle, so it's calm and cooperative and does not snarl as I warp the loom. I may dye the yarn or warp chains at this point as well so that the yarn is completely "finished" before I begin setting up the loom, which leads to fewer surprises when the fabric comes off the loom.

Yarns used as singles are typically called "active" yarns. In most cases, the twist needs to be controlled in order for them to be woven. Before I weave with singles, I usually "set" the twist with the aid of a yarn blocker. The blocker allows the yarn to dry under slight tension to encourage the yarn to dry flat (without stretching). This helps the yarn remain straight and not kink on itself when you're weaving. But the energy (and liveliness) returns as soon as the fabric undergoes the finishing process.

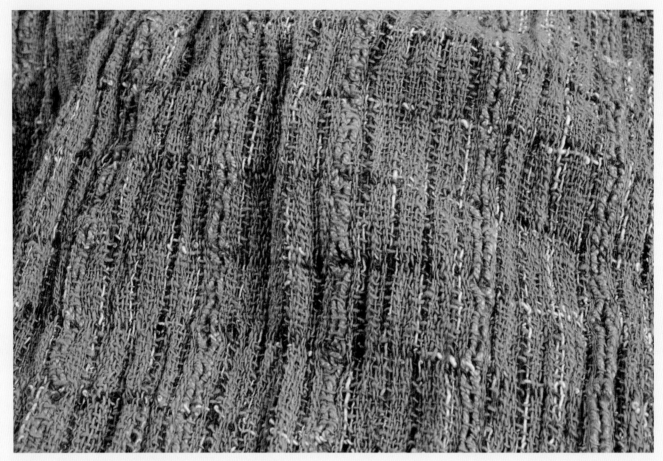

Stephenie Gaustad's Mostly Pink Leno Scarf (see page 118).

When I want a tightly twisted three-ply for rug warp or tablet weaving, I'll also wash the yarn and block it under tension. I wind the freshly spun yarn onto a PVC niddy-noddy, then plunge the whole thing into a tub of hot, soapy water. After rinsing thoroughly, I leave the yarn to dry under slight tension on the niddy-noddy.

If I wish to block singles yarns to be used in fabric weaving, I do so less strenuously. In these cases, I'll wind the wet (washed) yarn gently around a PVC yarn blocker (see page 137 to make your own). I pull the yarn tight enough to remove the slack but not so tight as to stretch it, then leave it to dry under this slight tension.

It's not always necessary to wash your handspun prior to weaving. Some weavers like working with yarn that has active twist, and they have techniques for handling it. I prefer to work with yarns that have been washed.

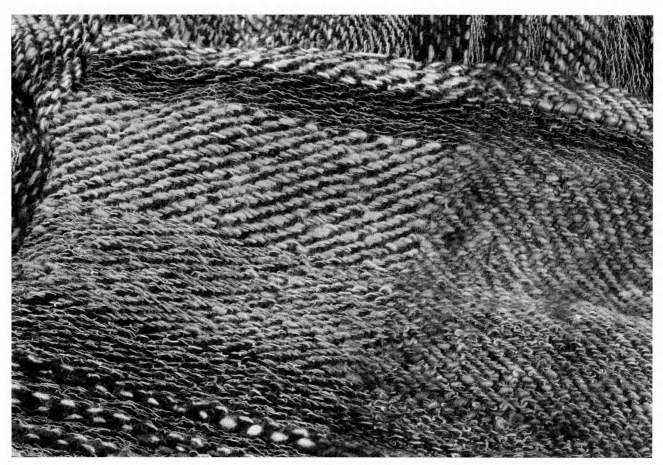

Yarns with varying twist amounts can produce interesting surface textures in fabrics. Kathryn Alexander's What Shoes Sock fabric (see page 122).

TO WASH OR Not to Wash

There may be times when washing the yarn prior to dressing the loom is not warranted: for a continuous warp, where there are not a lot of cut ends, for example, it's quite possible to work with unwashed yarns in the warp. Cut ends of freshly spun yarns can untwist, so when dressing a standard loom, the warp ends, which have to be cut to pass through the heddles and reed, are easier to use when finished prior to warping. In general, twist becomes stabilized in yarns that have been washed so that cut ends will not immediately unravel. The twist can also be set by steaming the yarns prior to dressing the loom.

I wove a series of eight samples using unwashed and washed two-ply wool yarns in plain weave and twill (see photos opposite) to see if there would be a difference between them after washing the woven fabric. As it turns out, I could discern no appreciable differences.

It can take considerable effort to secure the cut ends of an unfinished yarn when dressing a floor or table loom. Therefore, these samples are quite narrow so that I could thread the reed and heddles quickly. I alternated ends from two different skeins in both the warp and weft to balance any potential uneven twist and prevent variations in the way the yarns collapse in the finished fabrics. The unwashed yarns did shrink more in the finishing, but not so much as to cause appreciable differences in the finished fabrics. Given the difficulty of working with unwashed yarns, I don't think they are worth the bother.

Opposite, top: Plain-weave and twill samples woven with washed and unwashed yarns. Opposite, bottom: Finished fabric of the same samples. Notice the fuzzy appearance of the finished fabrics.

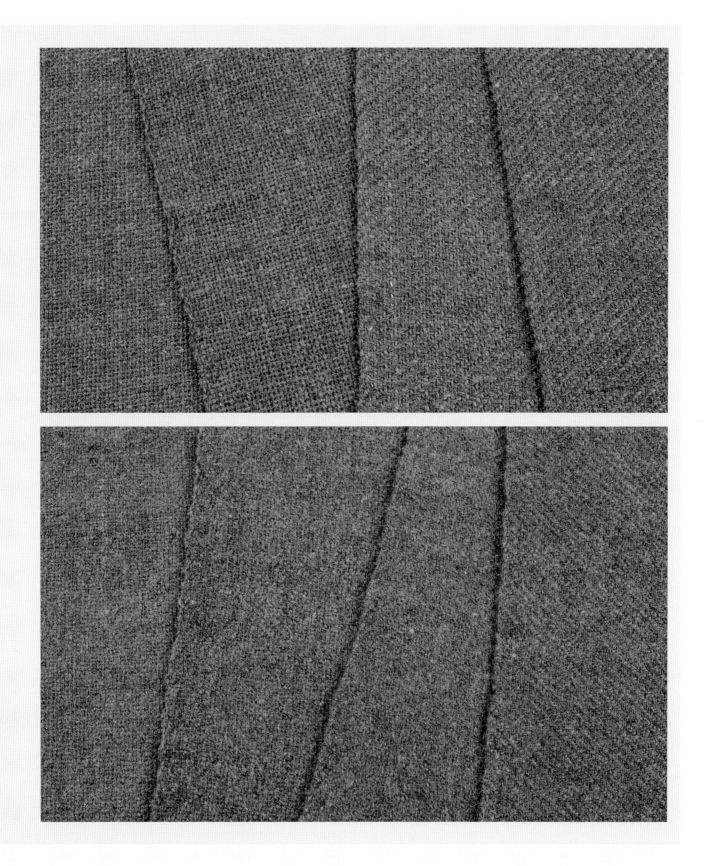

adding color

It seems that only another spinner cares if my fabric is hand-spun and only another weaver cares that it is handwoven. But just about everyone responds to the color. And as spinners, we have infinite color choices and many, many options for the way that we put color into our yarns. This flexibility leads to truly unique fabrics.

An array of natural colors can be blended for beautiful results. From left to right: alpaca shawl, angora/wool fabric, silk scarf.

Wool, silk, mohair, and alpaca come in many beautiful natural colors. Used individually or combined by carding or combing, a spinner can create any shade from white to off-white, golden yellow to brown, and light gray to midnight black.

But if it's color you're after, spinners have the full rainbow at their fingertips. We can purchase fleece that's already been dyed or dye it ourselves. We can add dye to any of the natural colors for subtle variations. We can ply together singles of different colors or we can blend colors within the roving or top before it is spun. The possibilities are wide and varied, as illustrated by the samples shown at right.

The options for dyers are staggering: natural dyes can be obtained from the kitchen and grown in the garden, plus there are exotic imported plants, animals, and minerals from all over the world. At the other end of the dye spectrum are commercially available manufactured dyestuffs (see Resources on page 134).

If you're new to dyeing, you might want to keep it simple. Try onion skins with an alum mordant or other things that may be in your kitchen right now—food color, drink mixes, and Easter egg dyes—that will impart color to fiber. All you need is a non-reactive pan, some measuring spoons, a spoon for stirring, and a heat source.

For protein fibers, I normally use a popular brand of dye powder sold as Sabraset or Lanaset. This kind of dye is both reliable and permanent. I want my long hours spinning, color planning, weaving, and sewing to be rewarded with colors that I expect and that will not fade or wash out.

I mix the dyes into a 1% solution (1 gram of dye powder for every 100 ml of water) and use a citric acid fixative (available at dye houses). Sometimes, I dye fibers in an immersion bath, in which the yarns are heated in a solution of water, dye, and fixative. For painted yarns or warps, I apply dyes and fixatives directly onto the wetted yarns, wrap them in plastic, and heat them in a tabletop stainless steel steamer.

You can purchase fiber that's already been dyed. From left to right: roving, top, locks.

The color in the yarn varies when the fibers are dyed prior to spinning.

I often choose to spin un-dyed fiber, then apply the color after the yarn is spun and ready for warping the loom. The yarn for the shawl shown on page 104 was spun from white bombyx silk. After winding the warp, I painted it with several shades of gold and violet to position the colors exactly where I wanted them. As a spinner, I can use the same colors to dye the fiber before it is spun into yarn. The fabric shown at the top of the photo below was woven from Bluefaced Leicester fiber that was dyed with the same shades of gold and violet. The same colors are used in a third sample but were spun as singles, then plied, either with the colors next to them in the fabric, or carded together before being spun. The different methods of applying color allow you many choices when planning the dyed fabric.

There are endless ways that the same colors can be used for different effects. In the sample shown at the bottom of the photo at right, the same colors are used as single-color stripes, single-color blends by alternating colors in warp ends (or weft picks), colors that are plied with their neighbors, and colors that are carded together with their neighbors. So, while the same colors are used, the way that those colors are used creates quite different fabrics.

The painted-warp sections in the two scarves at right were dyed with the same colors, but in one, the painted warp is surrounded by dark colors and in the other it is surrounded by light colors. The appearance and emphasis of the painted warp depends greatly on the other colors in the fabric.

Dyeing warp chains allows for color choices as well as color placement in the form of blocks of color along the length of the yarns.

There can be a more uniform look to the color variations if the fiber is dyed and thoroughly blended before the yarn is spun. The two fabrics shown here were spun and woven from the same dyed colors for two very different effects. The yarn in the upper fabric was spun from tops dyed several depths of shade of the same colors prior to spinning. The yarn in the lower fabric was spun from colors and depths of shade that were kept separate, spun separately, and then either plied as separate colors, or plied to visually blend the colors.

By painting dye onto a measured warp, you can dictate exactly where each color appears. The colors of the fabric at top were painted on the warp after spinning. The same colors were used to paint roving to make the color variation in the fabric at bottom.

The purple and copper along the left edge of this fabric are close in value and divided by a section where the two colors were carded together to make a smooth color transition. Other color transitions include thread-by-thread color blending in the warp and singles of two colors plied together for a blended color transition.

You can get even more variations by simply changing the order in which the same colors are blended. A thorough blending of many colors can produce a neutral background, as in the dyed-in-the-wool Merino samples shown at the top of page 51 that were blended before they were spun. This background allows the purple/fuchsia stripes to pop.

You can create heathered looks by overdyeing gray or brown fiber, as in the Shetland singles used for the tweed fabric shown at the bottom of page 51. Any fiber can be overdyed; using the same color over different natural colors will give you a range of depths of shade that will blend together nicely.

The appearance of any color depends on the surrounding colors. Both of these fabrics have stripes of the same rust/green painted warp but the stripes are adjacent to darker colors in the fabric on the left and they are adjacent to lighter colors in the fabric on the right.

A thorough blending of many colors can produce a more neutral background, as shown in this fabric. Fiber from Deb Menz.

For this vest fabric, I combined solid colors of fiber, dyed fiber, and some gray fiber that was overdyed with reds. See page 90 for the completed vest.

The way that you choose to spin dyed roving and top can affect how the colors appear. The Bluefaced Leicester/silk fabric shown at right was woven from a variety of dyed yarns using gradient-dyed top to give a series of non-repeating colors along the length, solid-color top that was painted as warp, painted top, and solid-color top dyed prior to spinning. For the larger or more dominant areas of color, I spin solid colors or I paint the warp after spinning. For more blended areas, which visually recede into the background of the fabric, I use dyed fibers or top. The blended fibers can include some of the colors of the solid or painted yarns, or they can be a distinct set of colors designed to highlight the solid colors.

For maximum blending of color, apply dye in small areas along the length of the top. Then divide the top into lengths measuring 12" to 18" (30.5 to 45.5 cm) or so. Split the lengths in half lengthwise, spin each separately, and then ply each with another section.

Combining yarns dyed with a variety of dye methods creates interesting color depth in the fabric.

Color can be achieved with pre–dyed roving or top.

For this alpaca/silk shawl, I spun one ply of the warp yarn end to end from a single dyed braid so that the color blocks were maintained. I then plied it with a semi-solid alpaca/ silk yarn of oranges and reds that doesn't interfere with the first ply's colors.

Hand-dyed fibers, either top or roving, typically have long sections of colors. If you want to preserve long lengths of color, spin the braid from one end to the other so that the yarn maintains the distinct color gradation of the painted fiber. If you want a plied yarn, choose a solid or semi-solid color that won't overshadow or confuse the original colors.

The same colors in color-blended top can be spun in different ways to add variation in the woven fabric. The samples shown at the top of page 54 were both woven from singles in the warp and weft, spun from the same batch of wool top. The sample on the right was spun from the end of the preparation, using the whole top; the sample on the left was spun from the fold, using sec-

tions pulled off in order, not aligned to separate the color changes at all. Notice how the end-feed method tends to homogenize the colors, while the fold technique leaves the colors more distinct. Clearly, the more dramatic the color changes in the top, the more dramatic the effect will be in the finished fabric.

If you decide that you don't love the color of the finished fabric, you can always overdye it. For example, I decided that the colors in the fabric shown at the bottom of page 54 were too bright, so I overdyed it with rust.

Two samples woven from the same color–blended top. Spun and woven by Carolyn Hart.

Occasionally I don't like the colors in a fabric once it is woven and I'll I tone down bright colors by overdyeing the fabric. Both of the fabrics shown here were woven on the same warp. The fabric on the bottom was overdyed with rust.

All of these fabrics are examples of how I've tried to duplicate the colors of a memorable sunset in my spinning and weaving.

Both of these fabrics were woven with the same warp and weft. The fabric on the left was overdyed. Much like watercolors produce layers of colors, dyes produce layers of color in fabric.

COLOR INSPIRATION

You can find ideas for color combinations and choices literally everywhere you look. Back in 1974, I took an early evening flight from Los Angeles to San Francisco. Out the window, I watched a haunting and memorable sunset of deep golds, reds, and dark navy-purple-blue. Even though I wasn't yet a weaver, spinner, or dyer, I went to a yarn store the next day in search of these colors. I found yarn that was close—but not exact—and I have spent many hours trying to recreate those colors through my spinning and weaving.

I like to peruse books on watercolor because dyeing is so similar to painting with watercolors. You create layers of color through which previous colors peek and affect the overall color impression. This helps me decide which colors to use when I overdye a fabric or yarns.

Use your garden, your vacations, or your interests to select color combinations that appeal to you, and buy, dye, or blend colors to represent what you see. Make your work personal, meaningful to you, and an exploration of colors that sing to you.

Once you have chosen a color or color family for a particular project, choose colors to complement, blend, or contrast with those colors for visual interest and variety. Refer to a painter's color wheel for monochromatic color schemes, complements (colors opposite each other on the color wheel), and analogous or triad colors. You'll learn a lot about color in *Color Works* (Interweave, 2004) by Deb Menz.

Lynn Harper turned to the purply blues and reds of fresh blackberries for the colors in her shawl (see page 128 for the entire shawl).

A color wheel is a useful tool for getting ideas for mixing and matching colors—
a good one will give you various depths of shade of each color and point you to
analogous colors (next to your color on the wheel) and complements (across the wheel
from your color) for help in choosing accents and coordinates when you are planning
color amounts and placement in your fabrics.

weaving

Weavers today can choose from a variety of well-made looms. I use a 32" (81.5 cm) eight-shaft jack-type floor loom made by Gilmore that I've had for more than thirty years. When things are going smoothly, I can weave somewhat unconsciously, free to watch the fabric develop and quickly catch any hang-ups in treadling or throwing the shuttle. If something is not right, I know what to look for and how to fix it. I don't have to try to remember, research, or call on another weaver to help me solve the issue. Knowing my tools and how to use them saves me endless hours of frustration.

SAMPLING TO CHOOSE SETT AND WEAVE STRUCTURE

Sett, or the spacing of the warp yarns in the reed, is determined by several factors—the size of yarn, the weave structure, and the desired hand or feel of the finished fabric. There is no perfect sett for any one yarn; choices will depend on what you wish to make with the fabric.

In weaving, the sett in the reed (measured as epi) is largely determined by the size of the warp yarn. Wrapping yarn on a gauge or ruler will give you a sense of the yarn's density. It may not be as accurate as measuring yards per pound, but if you are consistent in your wrapping, using the same tool and the same amount of tension when wrapping the yarn, you will get a base point from which to make calculations for your first sample.

In general, plain-weave fabrics are the most sturdy and cohesive, given a specific grist and sett. This is because there are no floats, or skips, of yarn in the plain-weave structure. The warp and weft are not captured as closely in twills, which makes them favored for fabrics where drape is desired. There is more movement of the warp and weft in twills, and the yarn relaxes more during finishing.

STANDARD Yarn Sizes

The size of weaving yarn is generally measured in yards per pound. Published sett charts give typical ranges of setts appropriate for yarns of different sizes based on the fiber and weave structure used. Another way to estimate setts is to measure the number of wraps per inch of the warp yarn—loosely wrap the yarn around a ruler or inch gauge and count the number of wraps in one inch (see page 40).

According to conventional sett charts, the number of wraps in one-half inch corresponds to an appropriate sett for plain-weave fabrics that use the same size yarn in both the warp and weft. The number of wraps in about two-thirds of an inch corresponds to an appropriate sett for twills, using yarn of the same grist for weft.

WARPING THE Loom

When using my handspun yarn, I like to warp my loom from the front to the back because I find it easiest to blend colors across the warp this way. The photos here show the process I used for the Alpaca/Silk Shawl shown on page 82.

To begin, slip the lease sticks through the cross and secure them to the front beam. Knot the warp bouts around bobbins to help keep the warp ends from slipping while you sley the reed and thread the heddles.

Sley the warp ends through the reed, arranging the colors as you choose. Start with the warp chain on one edge and continue from chain to chain, crossing over the previous chain if necessary, until all warp ends have been sleyed.

Once all the ends are sleyed through the reed, check for color balance, correct order, et cetera, by looking at the warp from the back (heddle) side of the reed.

Thread the heddles, tie onto the back apron bar, wind the warp onto the warp beam, and tie onto the front apron bar. Use a few shots of waste yarn to spread the warp, then insert waste yarn or lease sticks to set aside extra warp length for fringe (if needed) and begin weaving.

Sett

Just as there is no "right" needle size for knitting, there is no "right" sett for weaving a particular yarn. You can get an idea of an appropriate sett by comparing the grist (wpi) or yardage per pound of your handspun to a standard sett table. But don't rely on such tables to ultimately determine the best sett—handspun yarns can vary so widely from spinner to spinner, fiber to fiber, and preparation to preparation that it can be hard to make meaningful generalizations.

The only reliable way to determine the best sett for your handspun yarn is to weave samples at a range of setts, then wash and press the woven fabric and compare the samples. While you're going to the trouble, you might as well sample different weft yarns and weave structures. Most likely, several of the samples will indicate appropriate fabrics for a number of uses. The decision you ultimately make will be based on personal preference.

In many cases, you can allow for sampling by adding about a yard to the warp, then begin by experimenting with different setts, wefts, and weave structures on this extra length of warp. But sometimes, you may not have enough yarn to weave a sample and still have enough for your project. In these cases, it's a good idea to sample with a different yarn that has similar properties. Your samples won't reflect exactly what you'll get with your yarn, but you won't have sacrificed any of that yarn to weave the sample.

For the Pygora Hooded Scarf shown on page 62 (see also page 94), I knew that I didn't have enough extra yarn for a sample. But I knew that kid mohair behaves in much the same way as pygora and that a sample woven out of kid mohair would provide a good substitute. For both the pygora and mohair, I spun a fine two-ply with plenty of twist that would withstand brushing on the loom.

Both the pygora and kid mohair measured 18 wpi. I therefore sampled the kid mohair at three setts—12 epi at 18" (45.5 cm) wide, 15 epi at 14" (35.5 cm) wide, and 20 epi at 11" (28 cm) wide. For weft, I used

Bluefaced Leicester/Silk Tibetan Jacket detail of twill and weft samples (opposite top).

To estimate the correct sett for my limited amount of pygora, I wove samples with kid mohair—which has many of the same characteristics—at 12, 15, and 20 ends per inch, shown left to right (opposite bottom).

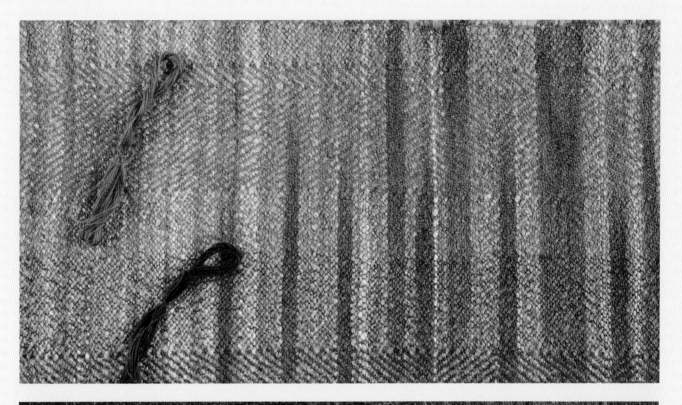

I sewed the kid mohair fabric (left) into a hooded scarf similar to the one I planned to make out of pygora (right). Here, the two fabrics are shown side by side.

a fine two-ply angora silk and brushed each sample lightly on the loom as I wove.

I left one sample of each sett unwashed, and washed a length of each to measure shrinkage and see how the fabrics differed in hand. The sample sett at 12 epi shifted a great deal and produced a fabric that was too open for my intentions. The sample sett at 15 epi looked just fine; the sample sett at 20 epi turned out stiff and dense. Because there was warp remaining on the loom, I decided to weave it off at a sett of 15 epi, then I washed and pressed it. Much to my surprise, the weft in that larger fabric shifted in the washing and ended up looking much the same as the 12-epi sample. Maybe I agitated the fabric more or my beat was less consistent, but I didn't care for the way the

fine weft shifted, though the fabric had a nice hand. I therefore decided to weave the pygora at 15 epi and use a soft but thicker weft that would have less room to shift as the fabric was finished. I chose a raw silk dyed in a variegated copper and red, which would also add a little color interest to the fabric.

I used the kid mohair fabric to make a mock-up of a hooded scarf. It was slightly wider than the pygora fabric would be, so I was able to make a deeper fold around the hood, but the two are quite the same.

CHOOSING THE WEFT FOR WARP-DOMINANT CLOTH

Weavers describe fabric as balanced if the same grist of yarn is used for warp and weft, with epi equal to ppi. Twills, huck lace, and many other fabrics are typically woven this way. But there are also countless ways to combine different yarns as a warp and weft, using different spacings so that one or the other dominates the look and feel of the fabric.

Most of my fabrics presented in this book are plain weave, in which I used a close sett for the warp and fewer picks per inch (ppi) in the weft, which is generally a finer yarn than the warp. This type of fabric tends to drape in the warp-wise direction, that is, along the length of the fabric, because the close-sett, heavier warp dominates the fewer picks and finer grist of the weft.

When I took a class on weaving fabrics for clothing, I learned to use a fine, relatively insignificant weft. In class, we wove a variety of balanced, weft-dominant, and warp-dominant fabrics. After the fabrics were finished, we handled them to decide the best use for each. The warp-dominant samples tended to have better lengthwise drape than the others, which I believe is more flattering when oriented lengthwise in a garment. In addition, warp-dominant plain-weave fabrics are easy to set up for weaving. All of the color and textural interest and effort is in the warp. Once the loom is warped, it's relatively quick work to weave the fabric: you need just one shuttle, one weft color, and there are fewer weft passes per inch than there are ends per inch in the warp.

For most of my fabrics, I put a lot of effort into the fiber choice, twist, grist, and color of the warp yarns. I typically use a close sett and weave warp-dominant plain weave or a simple twill in which the weft contributes very little to the overall fabric other than providing a structure to hold the warp together. This is especially true with my warp-painted fabrics. I don't want the size or color of the weft to interfere with visual interest I've painstakingly created in the warp.

Also, I simply prefer the aesthetics of warp-dominant plain-weave cloth.

The weft can influence the look and drape of a fabric as much as the warp. For the samples shown on page 64, I sampled three different wefts for the same warp—gold wool, purple wool, and dusty rose silk noil. The wools were both Nature Spun Fingering (about 10/2 in size) from Brown Sheep Company at 2,800 yd (2,560 m) per pound with a moderate twist. The silk noil was Soie Naturelle from Henry's Attic at 1,800 yd (1,646 m) per pound with a softer twist. Compared to the wool, the silk is more compressible and less likely to full as much in the finishing. Both yarns are recommended for knitting with U.S. size 3 (3.25 mm) needles, but the fiber composition and twist amounts make them very different in hand and finishing as weft yarns. I ultimately chose the two-ply softly spun silk noil for the fabric.

I typically weave samples to compare wefts, colors, and sizes, and to assess finishing issues, if there are any, before I start weaving a particular fabric. At the beginning of each warp, the yarns and I need to settle into a rhythm—until the tie-on knots pass over the breast beam and begin to wind around the cloth beam, the tension on the yarns shifts and adjusts, making for less-than stellar conditions, so I use this part of the warp to test different wefts. Unless I need to know potential finishing variations, I rarely cut

I typically use fine commercial yarn for the weft in my garment fabrics.

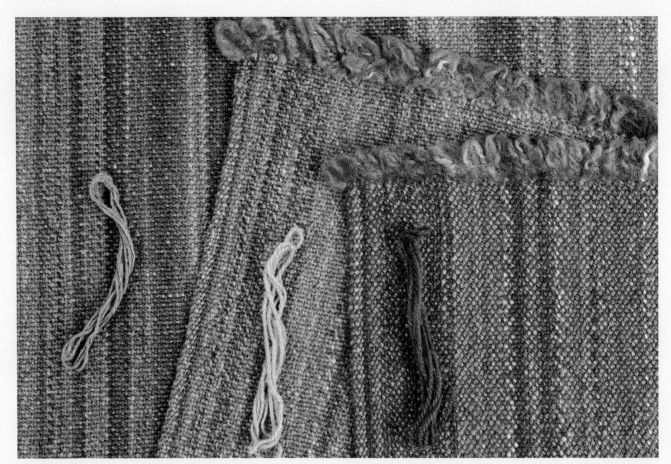

off these samples; I simply advance the warp and begin weaving the project. I add this part of the warp into the loom waste when calculating the number of yards I'll need for the warp (see sidebar on page 25).

In some cases, I let the end use dictate the type of weft I choose. For example, a heavy jacket might require a heavy weft. The three fabrics for a Tibetan jacket at the bottom of page 65 show three different weights of weft and fiber content—a softly spun woolen warp and weft at left, a firmly spun wool warp and weft in the center, and a firmly spun wool warp and commercial cotton weft at right. All three fabrics are suitable for the jacket pattern chosen, but for different levels of warmth. A variety of fabrics may be suitable for the same garment style, but the weight of the fabric will dictate the range of utility. For example, lightweight fabric is not as warm and while heavier weight fabrics are warmer and perhaps more durable, they are also bulky.

Weft choice can greatly influence the color and hand of a fabric. From left to right: dusty rose silk noil, gold wool, purple wool. I chose the silk noil weft for a comfortable lightweight fabric.

I typically sample an assortment of wefts at the beginning of each warp.

Weft choice can make very different fabrics from warps of the same grist and fiber. The warps here differ in color, but are otherwise similar in terms of grist and fiber.

FINISHING THE FABRIC

The fabric you see on the loom is not the finished fabric. Both the warp and weft are under tension and, if commercial yarns are involved, they might be coated with sizing compounds. You won't know what the fabric will really look and feel like until you remove it from the loom and wash it.

When you come to the end of your warp, secure the warp ends, remove the fabric from the loom, repair any mistakes, then wash the fabric. I wash every fabric that comes off the loom in the hottest water possible in my top-loading automatic washer equipped with an agitator column. I fill the tub with hot water, place the fabric in the tub (after the water has stopped running), and let it soak (without agitation) for at least twenty minutes. This allows the yarns to become thoroughly saturated. Then, I let the agitator run for about five minutes. I check the fabric and

decide if it is "done" or if it needs more agitation. In general, I want wool fabrics to begin to full and become more cohesive than the more open weave I see when the fabric is on the loom. There will also be a slight bloom or fibrillation on the surface of the fabrics, as the nap is raised in finishing. I check the fabric during this finishing wash, both by testing the warp and weft movement (can I slide the yarns in the weave structure?) and for evidence of surface fibrillation as the nap is raised.

Silk fabrics require longer agitation and soak times: the fibers take longer to absorb water, and I want them thoroughly shrunk in the finishing. I usually let them run through the whole agitation cycle, at least ten minutes. I keep a close eye on mohair, pygora, angora, and alpaca, which are prone to felting and require less time in agitation. I check at three minutes, and then again at five minutes, actually setting the timer, because these fibers can

The amount of finishing (washing and pressing) affects the look and hand of the fabric. From left to right in each photo: unwashed; washed for five minutes, pressed, and dried; washed for 10 minutes, pressed, and dried; washed for fifteen minutes, pressed, and dried.

MERINO. *Left to right: unwashed; 11% lengthwise shrinkage after five minutes of agitation; 13% after ten minutes; 14% after fifteen minutes.*

SUPERWASH MERINO. *Left to right: unwashed; 10% lengthwise shrinkage after five minutes of agitation; 10% after ten minutes; 10% after fifteen minutes.*

BLUEFACED LEICESTER. *Left to right: unwashed; 9% lengthwise shrinkage after five minutes of agitation; 12% after ten minutes; 12% after fifteen minutes.*

suddenly change from supple fabric to stiff fulled blankets in a flash.

When I am satisfied with the amount of agitation (and therefore, the amount of fulling), I'll set the washer on the final spin cycle (be sure that your washer doesn't add water during the spin cycle and inadvertently introduce more agitation) to remove the water. I then place the damp-dry fabric in the dryer on a hot setting for five or ten minutes, or until it is nearly dry, but not thoroughly dry. This helps to remove the large creases and fluff the fabric. The next step is to steam-press the fabric to remove the remaining creases. Pressing has to be done before the fabric dries completely or the creases will be permanent.

I press the fabric with a hot steam iron over a damp linen pressing cloth, being careful not to push the iron across the cloth, which can push the yarns out of alignment and distort the cloth. I slowly lower the iron onto the pressing cloth, press it down, then lift it and press it into the next section all along the length of one side of the fabric, then the other, continuing to press each side until the creases have all been removed. Silk, which seems to retain more

water after the quick-dry in the dryer, can require more pressing than wool or alpaca.

As a final step in finishing, I lay the pressed (and brushed) fabric on a flat surface or hang it over a 2" (5 cm) rod (I use a PVC pipe) suspended from the ceiling to dry fully. It's important that the fabric be allowed to lay or hang flat until it is thoroughly dry—any creases introduced by folds will become permanent if the fabric contains any moisture at all.

Different wools experience different amounts of shrinkage during finishing. Most of the shrinkage occurs during the first five minutes of washing, but longer agitation can increase shrinkage in some wools. Combining wools strand by strand, rather than in larger blocks, will help minimize differential shrinkage. The Merino/Bluefaced Leicester samples shown on page 69 have strand-by-strand combination warps at the bottom of each photo and distinct stripes of each wool in the upper section.

Brushing is a great way to raise the nap, or fibers, on the surface of the fabric. Brushing forces the fibrils (fine fibers)

CORMO. *Left to right: unwashed; 13% lengthwise shrinkage after five minutes of agitation; 13% after ten minutes; 13% after fifteen minutes.*

MERINO/BLUEFACED LEICESTER WARP WITH MERINO WEFT. *Left to right: unwashed; 12% shrinkage after five minutes of agitation; 13% after fifteen minutes.*

MERINO/BLUEFACED LEICESTER WARP WITH BLUEFACED LEICESTER WEFT. *Left to right: unwashed; 15% shrinkage after five minutes of agitation; 16% after fifteen minutes.*

to work their way out of the yarn and create a halo around the core of the yarn—or the surface of the fabric—in a process called fibrillation. There are several fibers that are suitable for brushing either during the weaving or finishing process, such as wool, mohair, angora, and alpaca. I would not brush silk or short fibers such as cotton, cashmere, or yak, because they will fibrillate on their own over time. Silk, not so much; but who wants fuzzy silk?

Because it is easiest to brush fabrics that are held under tension, many weavers choose to brush the top surface of the fabric (which is easier to access than the underside) as it is woven. The other side is usually brushed after the fabric is off the loom, during the pressing stage. I hold the warp end of the fabric taut with one hand as I brush in the opposite direction with the other, following the direction of the warp. When brushing during the finishing process, I continue to brush and press until the fabric has no creases and is nearly dry. For brushing, I have used a wire brush, a nylon hairbrush, and a flick carder. While all work well, I prefer to use a nylon hairbrush because it is comfortable and lightweight in my hand, it tends to be gentle on the fibers, and, most importantly, it doesn't cut the skin when I accidently brush my own hand.

Some fibers, such as angora, mohair, yak, or cashmere, will fibrillate during wear or use. When the fabric at right was first finished (without brushing), it looked smooth and crisp. One side was brushed to give an indication how it would fibrillate with wear. After sixteen years of wearing and use, both sides of the fabric have developed a pronounced halo that makes it so very soft and warm.

An assortment of brushes can be used to raise the nap on fabrics. From top to bottom: flick carder, wire brush, nylon hairbrush.

Angora will fibrillate and develop a halo with use. Both samples shown here are woven from a wool/angora blend. The folded fabric on top is just off the loom and brushed on one side. The fabric underneath is a shawl that I've used for 16 years, which has a much fuzzier appearance.

in summary

So what did I learn from spinning and weaving all of these samples? Mostly, that very nice fabric can be woven from everyday yarns. We might worry too much about twist and grist consistency, and fret over too many details such as how the fibers are positioned when the twist catches them or when plying two strands together or whether to wash or steam the yarns to set the twist. Fabric woven from handspun yarns has character; that's part of the beauty of it, the life in it, and too much control can erase these essential qualities.

I found spinning in the reverse direction much too fussy and annoying given the very limited effect on the types of plain-weave fabrics I like to weave. But I only sampled plain-weave and simple twill structures, so I can't evaluate if reverse-twist yarns might have more effect in other weave structures. There is much more work to be done!

Above all, relax. Twist variation balances out in the finished fabric as long as your yarn is reasonably consistent. Close examination of my yarns and fabrics will show inconsistencies, but they don't detract from the overall look and feel of the fabrics. Samples in which I intentionally wove high-twist and low-twist yarns together did not show a great deal of surface variation (see pages 30–31).

Adding color when using reverse-direction twist yarns has potential for further study.

Most of the two- and three-ply yarns used in the fabrics in this book were plied directly from the bobbins. I do not spin and then wind onto a storage bobbin for plying as a habit; I'll also wind off remainders from the last bobbins and ply them from both ends of the ball. Whenever I combined these plying variants as blocks in a warp, I kept track of where they were to evaluate possible variations in the nap, shrinkage, hand, or appearance of the yarns in the finished fabrics. I could tell no differences in my fabrics—the various yarns behaved the same in the finished fabrics.

Warp yarn is wound to and fro on a warping board or warping mill and the shuttle passes the weft back and forth across the cloth—in short, all yarns go all ways in woven fabric. Finishing the fabric erases minor traces of twist variation and amount in the spun yarns.

If we were dependent, as were our ancestors, on the yarns we spin and the cloth we weave to clothe ourselves and our families, we would work as efficiently and as expediently as we could. Long-draw spinning is a fast and efficient method of producing lots of yarn, and as long as there is ample twist inserted, it will hold up through weaving, finishing, and wearing. Because they are so durable, high-twist yarns actually improve with time and use.

High-twist yarns that are closely sett do produce surface interest in plain-weave fabric. You can exaggerate the twist amount to create special effects.

High- and low-twist yarns can be used together without a great deal of surface effect. Minor twist variation is usually not an issue.

CHAPTER TWO

use that yarn!
stories of fabrics

ONCE ALL OF THE BEAUTIFUL FIBER has been turned into luscious yarn, it's time to weave it into useful fabric. The samples in Chapter One have told us lots of things: twist amounts, sett choices, finishing choices, take-up, draw-in, and shrinkage rates. But we have to make the fabrics and, most importantly, use them to really learn if the project is a success. Beauty is only one part of a fiber or yarn's success; utility is another.

To illustrate the process of design, we'll follow the steps I use when I plan, spin, dye, and weave some garments. Because every spinner's yarn will be unique, reproducing the projects exactly is hardly the goal. But the process is the same, no matter what yarn you spin. My designs use the simplest of elements: smooth regular yarn, plain-weave fabric structure, and color. But there are many ways to use these few elements.

ᴗ*Alpaca*
SCARF

I INTENDED TO WEAVE ONE PROJECT IN ALPACA, but I ended up weaving three. The fibers are lovely to spin, they are warm (although a bit weighty, or heavy, compared to wool), and take color well in dyeing. For this blue/peach scarf, I began with two 4 oz (113 g) braids of dyed top that I had purchased because I liked the colors. Not having a plan made these the ideal fibers to try out first: I would spin, ply and measure the yardage, and plan a fabric to use it all. What I did not count on was the weight of the fiber: in most wools, 8 oz (226 g) is plenty for a shawl, but spun at this grist, I had just enough for a scarf, so that's what I made.

I split the top lengthwise and spun the two colors on four separate bobbins, then plied them together to create two skeins of two-ply yarn. I had 600 yd (549 m) of yarn that measured 20 wraps per inch (wpi), which is plenty for the warp of a scarf. I set the warp at 24 ends per inch (epi) for 8" (20.5 cm) in the reed and used a very fine two-ply silk weft in a dusty rose color.

The threading was straight draw; the fabric is warp-faced plain weave. The fabric is silky, drapey, and smooth. But this type of smooth fine yarn does not allow the fiber to trap air and provide as much warmth as I'd expect from alpaca. While the scarf is pretty and will be useful, it is heavier than I'd like and I think fabric of this weight would be better suited for a jacket or skirt.

The warp for this relatively dense scarf was smooth two-ply yarn spun from dyed top.

Natural-color *Alpaca*
SHAWL

NEXT, I MADE A SHAWL from various natural shades of alpaca roving. I started with 4 oz (113 g) of each of four natural colors of alpaca top: white, light brown, dark brown, and black from Lola's Loom (see Resources). I spun yarns that are lofty and have less twist per inch than the yarn I spun from top for the scarf so that the fabric would trap more air and add warmth. As I spun each color of roving for the warp, I was struck by how much the fibers differed. Some of the fibers were smooth and drafted like silk, while others were fuzzy and drafted like crimpy wool. The black fiber was the slickest and felt as if it would pull out of the yarn, even after finishing. The white fiber was the softest, the brown was soft but a bit sturdier, and the beige had the most fuzziness, or "tooth," which I was concerned might catch its neighbors during weaving.

Chosen for their natural colors, I tried to spin all of the fibers to the same grist and tried to impart similar twist throughout, although they had different staple lengths. I was concerned that some might stretch during weaving, so I sleyed the warp in random narrow stripes across the reed to help even out potential differential shrinkage. I warp my loom from the front, so I run each color as a separate warp chain, then spread each color out in a visually balanced way as I sley the reed. I save the last color (in this case, light beige) to fill in all the remaining spaces from side to side.

For weft, I used beige alpaca from Lola's Loom. There was only a small amount of each color available, so I spun two colors of beige fiber that were close in value, then plied them together for a soft two-ply yarn.

For this shawl, I used a variety of natural-colored alpaca. Each color had its own characteristics.

Both warp and weft were soft two-ply yarns that measured about 17 wpi.
I threaded 4 yd (3.6 m) of warp in a straight draw, alternating colors, at
15 epi for a 20" (51 cm) weaving width (300 ends in all). I wove plain
weave at 10 picks per inch (ppi). When taken off the loom, the fabric
measured 19¼" (49 cm) wide and had a woven length of 89" (226 cm),
excluding the fringe. I twisted and secured the fringe before I washed
the fabric. The finished fabric measures 19" (48.5 cm) wide and 84"
(213 cm) long, plus fringe.

There was not much shrinkage widthwise or lengthwise, which leads me
to believe that alpaca doesn't shrink as much as wool. Overall, the fabric
is warm and lofty but still seems distinctly heavier than wool fabric of the
same grist and size.

～Alpaca
SILK SHAWL

FOR THE THIRD ALPACA PIECE, I decided to introduce a silk blend to lighten the weight without compromising the inherent warmth and drape of the alpaca. I bought two 8 oz (226 g) braids of dyed alpaca/silk top for the warp that had long repeats of autumn colors from Abstract Fiber (see Resources) and another 8 oz (226 g) of a blend of baby alpaca and tussah silk that was dyed semi-solid analogous shades of reds and oranges from an Etsy shop, Violet Linx (see Resources). I spun the singles separately, ending up with almost 7 oz (198 g) of each color after sampling.

When I spin a blend of silk with wool or alpaca (or any fiber), I spin it as if it were silk: fine singles, with lots of twist in the plying. When using a fine fiber of any kind, I like to capture it in the yarn, so it has less chance to pill and fibrillate once the project is woven.

Like the natural-colored alpaca in the previous shawl, the fibers varied between the two preparations, so I plied them together. In addition to minimizing the possibility of differential shrinkage, this plying helped to preserve the color integrity of the dyed braid.

After plying, the warp yarn measured 20 wpi. I measured out 333 ends of 5 yd (4.6 m) each, which I sett at 15 epi in the reed for a 22" (56 cm) width. The long color repeats are seen to best advantage in a simple fabric, so I chose plain weave with a fine three-ply alpaca millspun lace knitting yarn weft woven at 14 ppi. I measured the warp extra long to allow for some sampling at the beginning.

For this shawl, I used a blend of alpaca and silk for the warp to produce a lightweight fabric with beautiful drape.

At the beginning of the warp, I wove and washed a sample to determine if the sett and weft choice would produce the fabric I wanted: lightweight but not too open. The weft finished well—it fulled nicely, fuzzed a little on the surface, and blended well with the colors in the warp without changing them significantly. An advantage of warp-dominant fabrics woven with fine wefts is that the fringe and the body of the fabric can look similar; in more balanced-weave structures, the warps can be so affected by the weft color that the fringe can appear to have little relation to the woven fabric.

After I removed the fabric from the loom, I twisted and secured the fringe. I then washed and pressed the fabric, brushed it lightly on both sides, and hung it to dry. The finished fabric measured 20" (51 cm) wide and 97" (246 cm) long, plus fringe. This shawl is very warm—fulling and brushing the fabric brought enough fiber to the surface to produce a nice halo.

Bluefaced Leicester/Silk
TIBETAN JACKET

FOR THE NEXT FABRIC, I wanted to use some Bluefaced Leicester and silk fiber that I purchased from Ashland Bay (see Resources) as a fundraiser for Breast Cancer Research. I had 12 oz (340 g) of a silver-gray fiber, and I spun a two-ply yarn that wrapped at 17 wpi. It was enough yardage by itself for a small project, but I found more of the same fiber, dyed, at The Spinning Loft (see Resources). So, I bought four more 4 oz (113 g) braids in two different colorways: two that were dyed as a long gradient from red to purple and two that were dyed a mix of colors including red, orange, purple, and copper. I also found a 4 oz (113 g) braid of dyed amethyst by Abstract Fiber (see Resources) and two 2 oz (56 g) braids of the same fiber dyed by Yarn Chef (see Resources) in bright oranges and reds. Because this added up to enough fiber for a large project, I decided to make myself a new jacket.

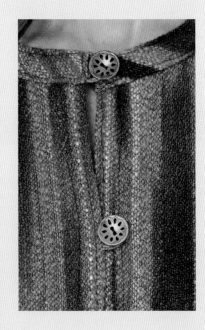

As for the Alpaca Silk Shawl, I spun the fiber as if it were silk: a fine singles, lots of twist, and tightly plied. I split the gradient top lengthwise and spun each half on a separate bobbin, then plied them together to produce long lengths of solid colors. I spun the spot-dyed fiber randomly without regard to where the colors would fall in the singles or plied yarn.

I split the other two braids of more solid colors (amethyst and reds) lengthwise and spun and plied them as separate colors. Finally, after winding the silver-gray yarns into warp chains, I painted them with colors similar to those used by the other dyers: reds, copper, and purple.

This jacket is an exercise in combining yarns spun from commercially dyed top and top that I dyed myself.

On average, the two-ply yarns measured 17 wpi. I measured several 8 yd (7.3 m) warp chains, totaling 270 ends, and sett them at 15 epi for an 18" (45.5 cm) width. I measured each of the five colors separately: one painted, one of oranges and reds, one spun from the red to purple gradient, one from the mixed color dyed braid, and one purple. I sleyed them through the reed individually, starting with the painted warp, then outlined those threads with purple and orange/red, placed the gradient along the outside edge of the fabric, and used the mixed-color dyed warp to fill in the remaining spaces. I chose this color placement so that the painted warp would run down the front/back and along the sleeves and not get lost in the side of the jacket.

I combined yarns spun from commercially dyed top and top that I dyed myself.

For weft, I used a fine two-ply wool (2/48 Merino) yarn from ColourMart (see Resources) that measured 44 wpi. This long warp ensured that I'd be able to sample different weft colors in both twill and plain weave and to weave an extra length of fabric to be fulled for comparison.

The weft-and-twill sample was revealing—the purple weft and twill structure completely dominated the warp colors and yarns. I liked the look of the rust weft better, but the twill structure still predominated. After spending all that time spinning and dyeing the warp yarns, I wanted them to be the focus of the fabric, not the weft or weave structure. Therefore, I chose to weave the rust weft in plain weave.

After weaving enough fabric for the jacket, I changed to dark purple weft and wove extra fabric at the end of the warp to sample for different finishing and fulling.

To finish the jacket fabric, I washed it, steam-pressed it, and hung it to dry. Because I wanted to use this fabric for outerwear, I agitated it longer than usual to produce a more cohesive fabric that would protect better from cold and wind. Keeping an eye on the agitation process, I fulled the fabric for a total of about ten minutes.

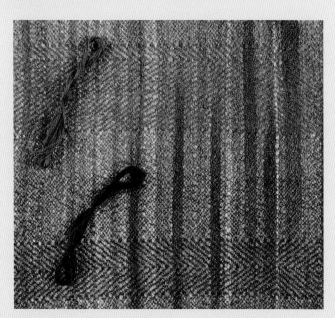

I sampled different weft colors in twill and plain-weave structures.

The finished fabric with the rust weft measured 14" (35.5 cm) wide and 4 yd (3.6 m) long; the fabric with purple weft measured the same width and 2½ yd (2.3 m) long. I re-washed the purple-weft sample to see if it would felt further—it did somewhat, but did not become really thick or firm. I plan to use it for a vest someday.

I cut and sewed the pieces according to the Tibetan pattern provided on page 141 and I lined it with commercial silk fabric.

After washing a second time, the purple-weft fabric only felted slightly (bottom). The fabric on top was washed only once.

I lined the jacket with commercial silk fabric.

I cut and sewed the pieces according to the Tibetan pattern on page 141.

~ Shetland
WOOL VEST

I AM FASCINATED BY THE COLLECTIONS and displays from different periods of history in museums. I look for both textiles and textile tools whenever I can and am astonished at the fine fabrics that were once produced with very simple tools and very little light to see by! I also like to read about the fibers used, weave structures, dyes, and how clothing was sewn. Because many fabrics are woven with singles, I ventured a bit outside my comfort zone for this vest and used handspun singles for both warp and weft. I chose Shetland wool, a fine fiber with lots of crimp, for its "sticky" nature that prevents it from raveling when cut (this yarn is traditionally used for steeked sweaters that are knitted in the round, then cut open along the center front and armholes).

I started with three 4 oz (113 g) braids of dyed Shetland fiber from Yarn Chef (see Resources). Once spun, I decided that the yarns would need to be grounded with a solid color to emphasize their similarities and prevent the colors from competing with each other, so I purchased 8 oz (226 g) of a semi-solid dark red Shetland in braids from Two Sisters Stringworks (see Resources).

Shetland wool fibers are full of crimp and texture, making them more likely to hold together and not slip past one another in a yarn. This makes it ideal for yarn spun into singles. To spin yarn with as consistent grist as possible, I stopped often and measured the twist angle to maintain a 20° angle in the Z direction and a grist of 20 wpi. I spun the singles a bit thicker than my usual yarns because it would have to stand on its own and I wanted to sett the fabric similarly to others that I weave.

Woven at a tight sett, this shawl fabric came off the loom quite stiff but became soft and drapey with use.

Knowing that singles can be un-
ruly during the weaving process,
I took care to wash and block both
the warp and weft yarns. To wash,
I dipped well-tied skeins into hot
water a few times, spun out the
water (on the spin cycle of my
washing machine), then wound
the damp (but not dripping)
yarn around a yarn blocker make
from PVC pipe (see page 137 for
construction plans). I wound each
hank separately on the blocker
and allowed each to dry for a day
before winding the yarn for use.
If you don't have space for a PVC
blocker, a PVC niddy-noddy
works just as well. After drying,
the yarn felt much more cohesive
than when I initially wound it off
the bobbins.

Shetland wool spun to the same final grist as the singles fabric in the Shetland Vest, but from two-ply instead of singles. The fabric is sett the same (20 epi), but is more sturdy and durable, and not as lofty, soft, or warm as the singles fabric.

For the warp, I sleyed one end of
red per dent in a 10-dent reed
for a 15" (38 cm) weaving width. Then I sleyed the four other colors in
sections across the width so that there were two ends per dent and an ef-
fective sett of 20 epi (300 warp ends total). Alternating the yarns in this
way meant that any variation between the yarns would spread out across
the full weaving width. Sleying the reed with the colors in this manner allowed me to "design in the reed," or choose how to spread out the colors
over the width of the fabric while I sleyed the reed. The process is easy to
do when warping from front to back, which is how I set up my loom for
all of the fabrics and samples in this book.

For the weft, I used a sixth color (natural gray) and wove it with two
shuttles, alternating them to help disperse any variations in twist or grist
there might be in the singles weft.

To weave, I threaded four shafts in a straight draw (1, 2, 3, 4, 1, 2, 3, 4,
etc.) and used a broken-twill treadling (1-3, 1-2, 2-4, 3-4). Simple twill
treadlings, in which each treadle change replaces one shaft with another,
can be less abrasive on the warp ends than plain weave, in which two
shafts are replaced with the opposite two shafts with each treadle change.
A straight twill treadling (1-2, 2-3, 3-4, 1-4) would also be less abrasive
than plain weave, but any unevenness in beat or grist would interrupt the
sharp diagonal twill lines and stand out like glaring mistakes. I was not so
confident of my yarn consistency to tempt the fates with a straight-twill
singles fabric.

To minimize abrasion, I beat each weft pick once on an open shed so that the weft wouldn't be squeezed over and under the warp ends as it was pushed into place with the beater, which could cause excess stress on both the warp and weft. Still, I had to fix at least four broken warp ends while weaving this cloth. Fortunately, twills (as well as plain weave) are easy structures to mend in the process of weaving. All of the warp ends that broke were dark red heather, which I thought felt harsher in my hands; I suspect this fiber had been distressed at some point. If I feel similar harshness in the future, I might look for a different batch of fiber. I think the yarns all broke at thin spots, where twist build-up made them more brittle, rather than from abrasion with their neighbors or beating. Maybe this red yarn was less evenly spun because the fiber was not as nice to handle.

After weaving, I treated the fabric in my usual man-ner—a hot-water soak, five minutes of agitation in the machine with a bit of laundry detergent, a quick run in the dryer, pressing, and hung to finish drying.

The woven fabric measured 14½" (37 cm) wide and 108" (274 cm) long. After finishing, it measured 13½" (34.5 cm) wide and 106" (269 cm) long, indicating 7% loss in width and a modest 2% loss in length. I expected more loss in length because the warp yarns had been blocked. But because it was blocked under even tension without stretching, I sur-mise that most of the lengthwise shrinkage occurred during the hot-water wash. There was no apparent tracking in this fabric, most likely because these are low-twist yarns and the sett and beat captured them enough in the weave structure to pre-clude movement during finishing.

The finished tweedy fabric was a bit thick for complicated tailoring, so I chose to make a simple vest that I adapted from a commercial pattern. The vest is fully lined with crisp silk and all edges are top-stitched to prevent raveling and rolling. I added iron-on interfacing to stabilize the buttons and machine-stitched buttonholes along the front edges.

To compare singles with two-ply yarn, I took some of the same fiber and spun two finer singles that I plied together and sett at the same epi. Both fabrics were made of the same fiber, wpi, and sett, but the singles fabric is decidedly more lofty, drapey, and fuzzy. It also feels less sturdy, but probably traps more warmth. I'll need to make a garment from the two-ply fabric to fully test the differences.

~ *Pygora*
HOODED SCARF

FOR THIS HOODED SCARF, I CHOSE PYGORA, a fine hair fiber that comes from goats. I had two 4 oz (113 g) batts of dyed fiber from Rainbow Farms Pygora (see Resources) that added up to enough for a scarf or small shawl. Because I had so little of this precious fiber, I decided to weave my samples with kid mohair (see samples on page 61), which is similar to pygora and which I had in abundance.

The two-ply pygora measured 18 wpi. I had enough of it for a 3 yd (2.7 m) warp sett at 15 epi for a 12¾" (32.5 cm) width. I started by sampling with two kinds of silk weft and chose to continue with Henry's Attic (see Resources) Soie Naturelle, a fine silk noil yarn that I dyed gold. The fabric is plain weave.

I brushed the fabric on the loom as I wove, stopping to brush both up and down in the warp direction each time I advanced the warp. I hemstitched both ends while the fabric was on the loom, then washed and finished the fabric as usual (see page 44). The brushed side was soft and fuzzy; the other side was less fuzzy, but still quite soft. The fuzziness will increase with wear over time.

In turning this fabric into a hooded scarf, I oriented the brushed side inward, toward the wearer's face. I folded the fabric in half, stitched the two sides together for 8" (20.5 cm) from the fold for the back seam, then folded the top corner down to the inside and stitched across the seam. I chose not to trim the excess fabric at the point of the hood; instead I just tacked it down. Then, I folded back the brim edge around the hood and stitched it in place to ensure that the selvedge edge didn't become floppy.

I brushed one side of the fabric, then oriented the brushed side so that it would be against the face in this pygora hooded scarf.

～ Tussah Silk
COLOR-BLEND SCARF

THIS TUSSAH SILK SCARF gave me the opportunity to explore color blending in three-ply yarns. I most commonly spin two-ply yarns and was interested in seeing the color possibilities that a third ply could introduce. I spun most of the yarn for this scarf on spindles while I was traveling. Consequently, the amount I spun of each color depended on how much fiber I had with me at the time. This made the project particularly fun—the color changes were plied together based on the colors I had with me. Because I spun the silk thin, I could pack small amounts of fiber and end up with lots of yardage on each spindle.

Color blending with three plies allows for subtle color shifts or interim colors between two highly contrasting colors. I began with 4 oz (113 g) of each color of pre-dyed silk top from Portland Fiber Gallery and Weaving Studio and Opulent Fiber (see Resources) in blue, burgundy, red, copper, and yellow. I blended the colors by plying in stages: three plies of blue; two plies of blue and one of burgundy; one ply of blue and two of burgundy; three plies of burgundy; two plies of burgundy and one of red; one ply of burgundy and two of red; three plies of red; two plies of red and one of copper; one ply of red and two of copper; three plies of copper; et cetera, for a total of seventeen three-ply combinations.

This scarf was an exercise in how colors can be blended in three-ply yarns.

The three-ply yarn measured 20 wpi, so I set it at 30 epi to ensure a warp-dominant fabric with plenty of warpwise drape. I measured the colors in individual warp sections, for a 3 yd (2.7 m) long warp that had between 7 and 40 ends of each of the 17 color combinations. I sleyed the reed from the front, arranging the colors across the fabric from darks to lights and then back to darks. When using a variety of unrelated colors: reds to golds to blues, I try to make the edges of the fabric be of similar colors and values so that the weft color will appear to tie it all together. For weft, I used a fine dark red commercial Merino/silk two-ply yarn from ColourMart (see Resources) that I beat at 16 ppi.

The resulting fabric is lovely—it's sturdy, firm, lustrous, and drapes very well. And, it should wear like iron, because the silk warp that dominates the fabric is tightly spun and plied. With a heavier weft, the fabric might give a rep-weave, or horizontal ribbed effect. In addition to being fun to spin and weave, this scarf has me anxious to try weaving four- and five-ply color-blended yarns. The color possibilities are staggering!

I varied the colors while plying the singles to create gradual color shifts.

～ bombyx
SILK SCARF
with painted warp

THIS BOMBYX SILK SCARF was woven from a firm two-ply yarn spun in white, then painted before weaving. While simple and fun, warp painting is a great way to learn to play with colors and proportion, and end up with coordinating fabrics.

For this scarf, I started with two bricks (10 oz; 283 g) of bombyx silk from Treenway Silks (see Resources). I spin silk for my projects over the course of many months, and I make an effort to maintain an even grist through-out. I spin top and bricks off the fold, which allows the fibers to draft smoothly from the side of the bundle with fewer clumps while I insert a tight twist. Toward the end of a bundle, the fiber will want to spin out of the mass of fibers rather than off the fold. But if held loosely, all the fibers will draft out properly. This spinning method firmly catches both ends of individual fibers and results in a smoother yarn. I find that if I try to spin from the end of silk tops, the leading end will not always get caught in the twist and the surface will appear fuzzy. Spun silk will always be slightly fuzzy, and certainly more so than reeled silk, so a tight twist helps catch all the ends in firmly.

For the warp in this scarf, I spun two-ply white bombyx silk, then painted it with dyes.

The two-ply warp yarn measured 40 wpi. I wanted a closely woven fabric, so I sett the yarn at 48 epi. I measured the plied yarn off the bobbins directly into warp chains, then washed them in preparation for dyeing. I spun two bobbins of singles, plied them together, and, when I had two bobbins plied, ran them together in a warp bout (a section of the total number of warp ends needed). Once I had enough bouts to make the fabric, I dyed and painted the warps. I mixed the dyes at a 1% solution and blended colors to produce shades of wine, deep purple, green, dark magenta, rust, copper, and scarlet. I used a purple weft in warp-dominant plain weave. When I finished weaving, I decided that the green provided too sharp a contrast to the other colors so I overdyed the whole fabric by immersing it in a 0.25% solution of copper to tone down the green and impart a more pleasing color story (see photo on page 54).

I paint a wet warp by using brushes to apply dye exactly where I want it.

~ *bombyx*
SILK SHAWL

SILK LIKES A CLOSE SETT AND A FIRM BEAT—the fibers relax as they are used and a sett that feels soft right after finishing will become limp and sleazy and not wear well. Although the fabric may feel stiff when it first comes off the loom, and even after it is first washed and pressed, it will soften and drape nicely with use. I wove the shawl shown here in 2006 and it still looks like new and is beautifully soft with amazing drape.

I spun the bombyx silk from Treenway Silks (see Resources) for this shawl slightly heavier than I did for the scarf on page 100. I therefore sett a 3 yd (2.7 m) warp at 40 epi for a 25¾" (65.5 cm) weaving width (1,028 ends total). For weft, I used a commercial 16/2 unmercerized cotton in purple. After weaving, the fabric measured 25" (63.5 cm) wide and 76" (193 cm) long, plus fringe. I twisted and secured the fringe, then washed, pressed, and hung the fabric to dry, after which, the body of the shawl measured 72" (183 cm) long. Like a well-worn shirt or pair of jeans, the fabric has softened and grown more comfortable with use. I take this shawl with me whenever I travel; it gets shoved in and out of my tote bag and has been used as a pillow as well as an umbrella. It just keeps getting better!

Woven at a tight sett, this shawl fabric came off the loom quite stiff but became soft and drapey with use.

~ Tussah
SILK KIMONO

I HAVE MADE SEVERAL KIMONOS from cultivated bombyx silk with very good results. For this version, I decided to try wild, or tussah, silk, which has a characteristic golden color that results from the silkworm's diet of oak leaves. The color and quality of the fiber can vary depending on the climate and conditions under which the moths were raised. There are several types of wild silk moths, the most common being *Antheraea pernyi*, which is native to China, but rarely will you know which breed is responsible for a particular silk top.

Whereas bombyx fiber is exceedingly smooth, tussah is characterized by surface divots or irregularities in the fibers themselves that give it "tooth." The fibers tend to be a bit sticky and do not slip quite as easily as they are spun. The irregularities make it sparkle rather than shine the way that bombyx does.

I spun the tussah silk from Ashland Bay (see Resources) into a two-ply yarn that measured 38 wpi, which was slightly heavier than the yarn I spun for the scarf on page 100, which measured 40 wpi. I spun two bobbins of silk, plied them together, and wound 8 yd (7.3 m) warp sections of varying numbers of ends until I had enough spun and wound for the width of fabric I wanted.

I painted several of the warp bundles in analogous colors in values of copper by mixing gold and red violet in a 90/10 blend and a 75/25 blend, then diluting both colors for three depths of shade: full strength (dark), 50% strength (medium), and 0.1% strength (very light). I then resist-dyed some of the warp ends by tying off sections to prevent the dye from penetrating certain areas (called bind-resist or ikat dyeing). I also

For this kimono, I used a variety of methods to dye handspun tussah silk.

used braid-resist dyeing, in which I tightly braided three warp bundles together before dyeing them. For both types of resist dyeing, I painted the same analogous colors as before to produce a nearly monochromatic cloth. I also dyed a few sections in blue and orange for contrast.

I sett the warp at 40 epi for a 15" (38 cm) width (600 ends total), arranging the colors as I sleyed the reed. The generous 8 yd (7.3 m) length allowed me to sample wefts and weave structures; it also ensured that there would be some fabric left over after the garment pieces were cut out.

Through experience, I have learned to choose a weft that won't slide along the warp after the fabric is woven for garments that will not be stabilized with a lining or interfacing. If the weft is inclined to shift in fabric, the fabric can separate along seams, leaving gaps of unwoven warp or weft. Because I didn't plan to line this jacket, I knew I needed a "sticky" weft, such as fuzzy wool, unmercerized cotton, or raw silk.

After dressing my loom, I sampled a couple of wefts and weave structures to see which I'd like best. First, I used 16/2 unmercerized cotton weft in both plain weave and broken twill. I decided that the purple was too dark and contrasted too sharply with the overall color of the warp. I preferred the plain weave to broken twill structure because the twill obscured the effort I put into dyeing the warp. Next, I tried a weft of caramel-colored 20/1 tussah silk from ColourMart (see Resources) in

The sample I wove at the beginning of the warp allowed me to try 16/2 cotton weft in both plain weave and broken twill and 20/1 tussah silk in plain weave with a double and single beat. I chose to use plain weave, the finer weft in gold silk, and a double beat for the length of the fabric.

Detail of kimono yarn and fabric.

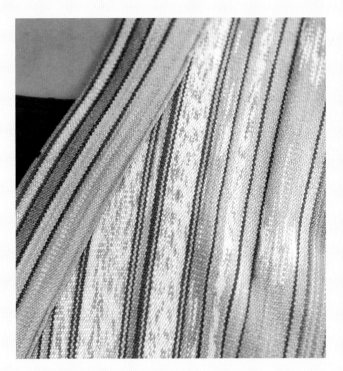

plain weave, woven with a double beat (beating once on the open shed, then again after changing the shed), then with just a single beat. I liked the size of the weft in both cases, but I preferred the firm cloth achieved by a double beat. After cutting the sample off the loom, I washed and pressed it to confirm my decisions. From this 3" (7.5 cm) sample, I determined the size and color of the weft, the weave structure, and how hard to beat the fabric. No wonder I'm a fan of sampling!

The woven fabric measured 14¾" (37.5 cm) wide. After washing, pressing, and hanging it to dry, it measured 13⅞" (35 cm) wide, indicating about 8% loss in width.

Having made this garment several times, I am accustomed to thinking of color placement and where it will land in the final garment. Although the fabric was decidedly asymmetrical, I knew that it would become harmonious when cut into pieces that were sewn together. Keep in mind that kimono-type garments hang best on someone with straight shoulders. You may find that too much fabric gathers under your arms if there is much slope to your shoulders.

The cutting and assembly instructions are available on page 138. I prefer to weave a separate fabric for the neckband so it has two selvedges and there is less need to finish the edges. I used the same tussah silk warp and 20/1 silk weft sett at 40 epi at a width of 5" (12.5 cm) for a total of 200 ends. To ensure I'd end up with the necessary 65" (165 cm) of finished cloth, I made the neckband warp 4 yd (3.6 m) long.

Knotted pile
AND *band-woven bag*

TO ILLUSTRATE HANDSPUN YARNS of a different character than those used for most clothing fabric, I wove a knotted pile bag (see *Woven Treasures* [Interweave, 2009] for more on weaving pile). The sturdy yarns used for bags, rugs, tapestries, and bands are typically spun from fibers with long staple lengths, such as longwools, mohair, or silk. The warps (and sometimes the wefts) are generally firmly spun and may consist of three or more plies.

All the yarns for this bag were spun of the same wool and mohair blend: a coarse wool, Romney in this case, blended with adult mohair at about 80% wool to 20% mohair. I keep lots of this fiber on hand for spinning warps, bands, and pile yarn. I spin it white, then dye as much of the spun yarn as I need for any given project. For the warp of the bag shown here, I spun a firmly twisted z3s (see page 30). Although the warp is completely covered by the knotted pile, it needed to be sturdy and withstand the abrasion necessary to create the weft-faced fabric. I used the same yarn for the edgings and the decorative soumak and twining along the top of the bag. For the strap, I used a finer two-ply spun from the same wool/mohair blend.

I used the same fibers for the pile weft but spun it much more loosely so that it would "bloom" and create the plush surface characteristic of knotted pile weaves.

Woven with knotted pile, this bag is an example of how handspun longwool can be used in fabric.

The velvet lining closes with a drawstring.

The soumak edge contrasts nicely with the purple velvet lining.

I set the warp at 16 epi across a 25" (63.5 cm) width to accommodate eight knots per inch on my upright rug loom. I needed 2,400 yd of three-ply for the 6 yd (5.5 m) warp: 25" × 16 epi × 6 yd. The project did not use the entire warp, but my loom has two fixed beams that require 6 yd (5.5 m) warp lengths. I usually plan to weave more than one bag from a single warp.

Typically, as I spin yarn for pile weft, I'll dye one or two skeins at a time. I keep records of the weight and yardage of each skein and how much dye was used, so, if I run out, I can dye more. It's not onerous to spin and dye the pile yarn; in fact, the project uses surprisingly little yarn. There are about 28,000 knots in the bag in five colors: 12,510 orange, 2,072 gold, 285 light orange, 7,552 dark blue, 3,944 light blue, and 1,637 white. Given that I use about 1"

The base is composed of five triangular sections.

(2.5 cm) of yarn per knot and I allow for some waste and errors, I figured that I would need at least 350 yd (320 m) of orange pile yarn and less for each of the other colors.

I spun the foundation weft in a fine two-ply from the same wool/mohair blend fiber. I also used the same yarn for the band, so I dyed some after it was spun.

Once I thought I had enough yarn, I started weaving. I have never yet run out of yarn in the middle of a bag project, but these are small weavings that take very little yarn. I wove the body as a single piece that included a long rectangle for the sides and five triangular shapes for the bottom. After removing the bag from the loom, I secured the ends with a half-Damascus edge. To finish, I gave the fabric a hot-water bath, then squeezed it between two towels to remove excess water, and laid it flat to dry.

I assembled the bag by inserting the band into the side seam, leaving a short tail on the inside that I sewed to the selvedge. Then I sewed the side seam and folded the triangle shapes and stitched them together to create the circular base. I used a buttonhole stitch to secure the band to one side of the top, sewed it down on the other side, and added a velvet edge to the top and a lining with a drawstring to keep the contents secure.

The selvedges, soumak, and twining were woven with the same sturdy three-ply yarn that I used for the warp.

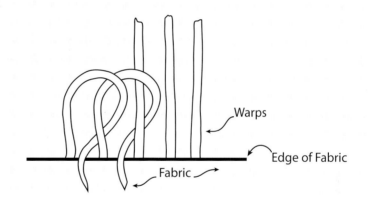

Warps

Edge of Fabric

Fabric

HALF-DAMASCUS EDGE. *Working with a pair of warps: fold the first warp end over its neighbor, behind, around, and bring the end back to the front between the two warps. Tug to secure. Repeat across the warp.*

CHAPTER THREE
gallery
of handspun fabrics

THERE ARE MANY SPINNERS WHO WEAVE, using different process-es to produce a wide variety of textiles. Every spinner has unique intentions when choosing fibers, preparing those fibers, and spinning them into yarns for weaving. I have invited friends and colleagues to present their textiles on the following pages to provide a more complete picture of the ways in which hand-spun yarns are used for weaving. These projects are presented for inspiration: most of these spinner/weavers have works in other publications if you wish to learn more.

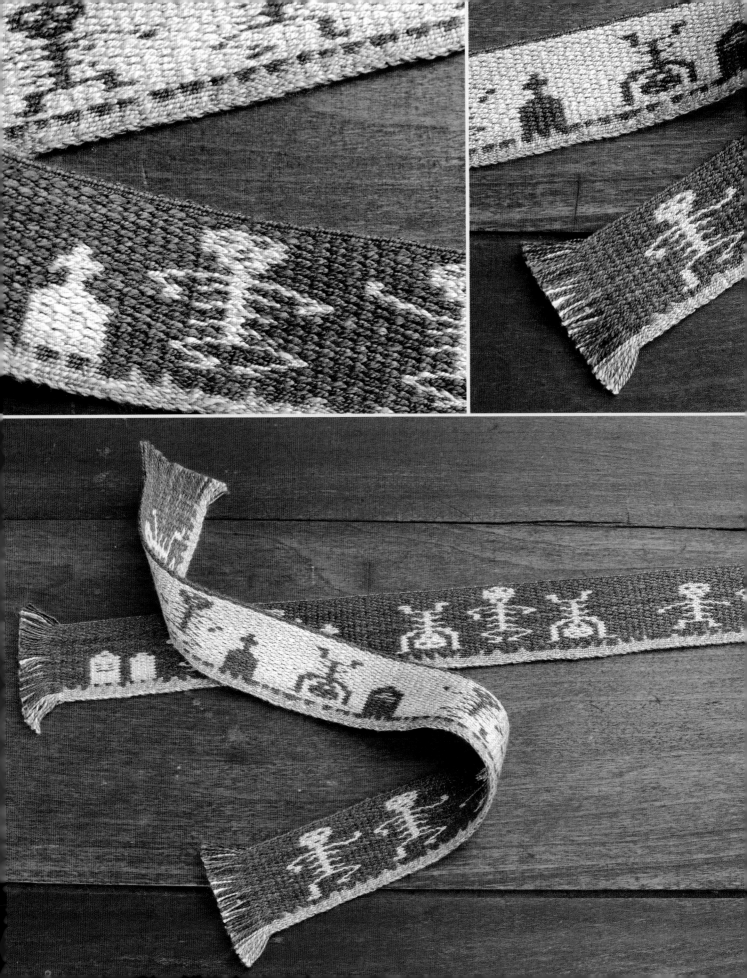

❦ Boneyarn
BOOGIE STRAP

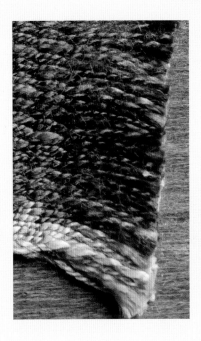

by **John Mullarkey**

For this whimsical portrayal of a graveyard party after dark, John Mullarkey spun hand-dyed bombyx silk top from Chasing Rainbows. With the aid of a super fast flyer head on his Lendrum wheel, he spun very fine yarn that approximated commercial size 30/2 silk. Instead of weaving the straps on a loom, John used a tablet-weaving technique to produce this original double-sided pattern—what's dark on one side is light on the other.

John Mullarkey has been tablet weaving and spinning for more than seven years. He has developed software, freely available on his website, for designing tablet-weaving patterns. He is primary author of A Tablet Weaver's Pattern Book *and his work is currently on display in the Missouri History Museum. Garments featuring John's tablet-woven bands have appeared in national and international fashion shows and have been published in* Handwoven *magazine. His ongoing mission is to find the perfect tablet-weaving loom for this loom-less art. For more information, visit malarkycrafts.com.*

FINISHED DIMENSIONS
1⅛" (2.9 cm) wide and 12" (30.5 cm) long, including fringe.

⌇ *Mostly pink*
LENO SCARF

by Stephenie Gaustad

Stephenie Gaustad's lightweight cotton scarf is a play of collapsed plain weave and doup leno openwork (see a close-up on page 42). She combined handspun rose cotton singles at 8,700 yd (7,955 m) per pound and space-dyed indigo cotton singles at 3,850 yd (3,520 m) per pound with commercial 5/2 pearl cotton in gray. Stephenie sett the yarns at 20 ends per inch in a 5-dent reed, skipping a dent between every pair of pearl cotton leno warp ends. The leno structure twists and untwists across the width of the cloth and the highly twisted singles collapse in between. This scarf was spun and woven in 1993: the twist energy is still active twenty years later!

For more weaving details, see the May/June 1993 issue of *Handwoven* magazine.

Stephenie Gaustad is well known to her fans and readership as a contributor to Handwoven, Spin·Off, *and* Jane Austen Knits. *Nothing delights her more than finishing a fine handspun, handwoven garment or the intricate details of replicating ancient cloth. An avid colorist and master dyer as well, Stephenie pursues the craft with frequent diversions into illustration, teaching, and writing.*

FINISHED DIMENSIONS
8½" (21.5 cm) wide and 66" (168 cm) long, including fringe.

ᔰ Casting off
tapestry BOOK

by Sarah Swett

For this tapestry book, Sarah Swett began with gray Romney fleece that she washed, teased, drum-carded, and spun (on a 40-gram spindle) into high-twist singles at about 4,800 yd (4,389 m) per pound. She plied each cop to itself for balanced two-ply yarn at about 2,400 yd (2,194 m) per pound for the warp. Using a simple frame loom made from plumbing pipe, she sett this warp doubled at 9 ends per inch. For the weft, she used softly spun singles wool from a variety of local fleeces spun at about 2,000 yd (1,829 m) per pound. She dyed the yarn with indigo, cochineal, madder, weld, or walnut with an alum/tartar mordant. This seemingly limited palette allows for endless color variations made possible by overdyeing, blending dyes in the pot, and starting with fleeces of different colors and breeds.

Sarah wove with two weft strands—usually of different colors—held together, changing the blends to create gradual shifts in both color and value and weaving in the ends as she went along. The result was a neatly finished and sturdy fabric with the front and back nearly indistinguishable—ideal for her book format.

Sarah Swett has devoted the last decade, or three, to telling slow stories with handspun yarn. While her tapestries and sweaters travel the world, she does her best to stay at home and do all her favorite things at once: spin, weave, read, knit, write, walk, drink tea, and play the fiddle. She thinks this may keep her occupied for some time to come. Visit Sarah at sarah-swett.com.

FINISHED DIMENSIONS
10" (25.5 cm) wide, 10" (25.5 cm) long, and 1¾" (4.5 cm) deep; each page measures 9" (23 cm) square.

What shoes sock

COLLAPSE CLOTH

by Kathryn Alexander and Carol Lee Shanks

This top represents artful collaboration between Kathryn Alexander and Carol Lee Shanks. For the cloth, Kathryn dyed and spun longwools, silks, Merino, and alpaca into energized singles that she then wove unfinished, without washing or steaming the yarns, at setts that ranged from 10 to 32 ends per inch. She wove plain weave and assorted twill patterns to form stripes or subtle patterns in a collapsed fabric. Carol examined the cloth for all of its nuances, then chose where to cut and how to sew pieces together, working the different areas of the fabric to their best advantage, finally ending up with the garment you see here.

An internationally known textile artist, Kathryn Alexander spins, weaves, dyes, and knits. Her work is characterized by an abundance of color, richly textured surfaces, and whimsical designs. She uses her ability to make yarns as the focus of all her cloth. This knowledge lets her manipulate the surface of woven and knitted fabric, in which she turns the physics of yarn into the main element of her designs. Kathryn lives in upstate New York, where she gardens and rides her horses when she is not working in her studio.

Carol Lee Shanks has a degree in textile and costume design from the University of California at Davis. She designs and handcrafts clothing and textile art pieces. An integral part of her work is manipulating cloth to create different surface textures. By layering opaque and transparent elements and then stitching, piercing, and wrapping them, she transforms linear shapes into dimensional silhouettes that become moving sculpture when suspended on the body or within a room. Carol works and exhibits her clothing and textile art at her studio in Berkeley, California.

~ *Forest*
LATTICE SCARF

by **Amy Norris**

For the warp of this scarf, Amy Norris spun dyed Lambspun Merino top and 80/20 Merino/silk from an unknown source. She spun and plied each on her Lendrum folding wheel at 10:1 ratios. For the weft, she spun Sanguine Gryphon variegated 80/20 Merino/silk top, also at 10:1 spinning and plying ratios. She then wove the scarf following Repeat Twill #411 pattern in *A Weaver's Book of 8-Shaft Patterns: From the Friends of Handwoven*, edited by Carol Strickler.

Amy Norris was introduced to weaving when she visited Greenfield Village as a young child, but she didn't start weaving herself until 1986. She now owns multiple multshaft looms and is an active member of many organizations, including the Weavers Guild of St. Louis, Complex Weavers, and WeaveTech. Amy finds excitement in marrying color and weave structure in ways that enhance both attributes. Amy's color studies often end up in dish towels woven of 8/2 cotton.

FINISHED DIMENSIONS
6¼" (16 cm) wide and 79" (200 cm) long.

⌁ Grandmother/Granddaughter
TEA COZIES

by **Denny McMillan**

Inspired by a children's book that culminates in a grandmother and granddaughter sharing pots of tea after a walk in the woods, Denny McMillan wove a duo of tea cozies inspired by the colors of a woodland retreat. Denny spun pre-dyed commercially prepared wool fibers into an assortment of weights of singles (with perhaps a bit of two-ply) on her Little Gem Maja Craft wheel. She sleyed the yarns randomly in her 10" (25.5 cm) Cricket loom and used a single color for weft. Denny added a vintage lining and stuffed the cozies with wool roving. She finished it off with the leftover handspun yarn.

Denny McMillan makes things in her hometown of Toronto, Ontario. She spins, weaves, knits, crochets, sews, and teaches all things fiber. Her family of two teenage boys and a patient husband look the other way as ever more yarn, fabric, and fleece appear in her already-full home studio. Denny is never bored.

FINISHED DIMENSIONS
large cozy: 12½" (31.5 cm) wide and 9" (23 cm) tall, including ruffle.

small cozy: 9¾" (25 cm) wide and 7" (18 cm) tall.

❧ *Blackberry*
SHAWL

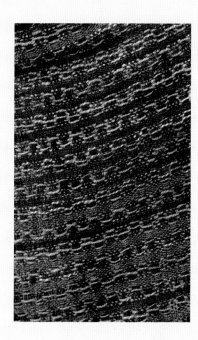

by Lynn Harper

While picking blackberries with her friends in August 2008, Lynn Harper snapped a few pictures of the blackberry patch, which became the inspiration for this shawl (see a close-up on page 56). She began by spinning yarns based on the colors in the photo—dark purple for the ripe berries, rosy-pink for the unripe ones, and green for the vines and leaves. She spun a total of 16 oz (454 g) of a variety of pre-dyed Merino/angora/silk, alpaca/Merino/silk, and Bluefaced Leicester/silk rovings and tops, overdyeing some of the yarns as necessary to achieve the colors in the photo. Using her Schacht Matchless wheel, she spun all the fibers into two-ply, heavy laceweight yarn that measured between 23 and 26 wraps per inch.

Lynn wove the shawl on her 50+-year-old four-shaft Purrington counter-balance loom, setting the plain-weave sections of the spaced-and-crammed warp at 12 ends per inch for about 24" (61 cm) wide in the reed and a length of 76" (193 cm). Once off the loom, she twisted the fringe, washed the shawl in warm water, and laid it flat to dry.

A conservation biologist in her day job, Lynn Harper has worked with fiber obsessively since she was eight years old. She knits, she spins, she weaves, and she claims that it is simply not true that her stash is one of the Seven Wonders of the World.

FINISHED DIMENSIONS
18½" (47 cm) wide and 71" (180 cm) long, including fringe.

glossary
of spinning AND weaving terms

a

active twist: twist that is not relaxed; usually fresh yarns or energized (highly spun) yarns have active twist.

b

backward draw: see long draw.

balanced weave: fabric in which the number of warps per inch is the same as the number of wefts per inch.

balanced yarn: yarn that has no obvious twist direction; achieved by relaxing during finishing or by removing and balancing twist during plying.

batt: a carded preparation from hand cards, a drum carder, or a carding machine.

beaming: winding the warp threads onto the warp beam; part of the process of warping the loom.

beat: to push the new row of weft against the previously woven row.

beater: a frame that holds the reed (the part that separates the warp threads); it is attached to the loom by an upright on each side that pivots or is hung from a structure above the loom.

boat shuttle: a wooden shuttle that looks a bit like a boat with a central hinged rod on which a bobbin (a slender spool) wound with the weft thread is placed; the bobbin rotates as the shuttle is thrown and the weft is pulled snug at the selvedge by the drag of the unwinding thread against the rotating bobbin.

bobbin: (*in spinning*) the storage unit for newly spun yarns; (*in weaving*) the storage and delivery unit for yarns to be wound off the shuttle.

braid: roving or top that has been braided to keep it orderly before spinning.

brick: a folded square form of silk top, usually 5–6 oz (142–170 g) per brick.

bubble: to add a slight curve in the weft before beating to prevent the selvedge from becoming distorted.

c

collapsed warp/weft: the result of using energized yarns that relax (collapse) in the finishing process to create surface texture.

crimp: the waves along the staple length of wool; crimp varies by breed.

d

dent: the spaces on a reed through which the warps are threaded.

differential shrinkage: the result of combining fibers that shrink more or less in the finishing or washing process.

direction of twist: either S- or Z-twist, depending on the direction the fibers were spun.

double-draft long draw: drafting a length of fibers, then attenuating against the twist until the yarn becomes stable along its length.

double-drive mechanism: a doubled drive band turns both the flyer and the bobbin at different rates so the newly spun yarn will be automatically wound onto the bobbin.

doup leno: a weave structure using a long string heddle (doup) to move a warp end from one location to another horizontally in the warp.

draft: (*in weaving*) a written plan for threading the loom; (*in spinning*) to attenuate and space the fibers along the length of yarn as it is being spun.

drafting triangle: the space between newly spun yarn and the fiber supply; it usually forms a triangular shape.

draw-in: the difference in width between the fabric and the warp in the reed; some weave structures draw in more than others.

drive band: a string or elastic band that allows the drive wheel to turn a smaller whorl on the bobbin, the flyer, or both.

e

end: one strand of the warp.

end-feed shuttle: a shuttle with a shaft secured at one end that supports a pirn (like a bobbin but with narrower end); the weft is pulled off the narrow end of the non-rotating pirn and tensioned with an adjustable tensioning device at the nose of the shuttle.

ends per inch (epi): the number of warps per inch in the reed or fabric.

energized yarn: yarn that has active twist energy.

f

fell: the woven edge of the cloth on the loom where the most recent pick has been inserted.

fibrillation: ends of fibers that escape from twist or weave structure and lie on the surface of yarn or fabric to make it fuzzy.

finish: *(in spinning)* setting the twist in a yarn, sometimes by blocking; *(in weaving)* after fabric is woven and cut off the loom, the act of washing, pressing, raising the nap, and hanging it to dry.

forward draw: using one hand to pull fibers forward toward the emerging yarn while holding the package of unspun fibers stationary.

forward hand: the hand held toward the orifice in wheel spinning.

fulling: vigorous washing that causes the fibers in the fabric to become cohesive.

g

gradient dyeing: dyeing colors that merge gradually from one to another along the length of fiber or yarns (vs spots of colors).

grist: a measurement of the yardage and weight, usually given as yards per pound; heavier grist means a denser and fatter yarn with fewer yards per pound.

h

hand: how fabric feels; usually described after washing and pressing.

hand beater: a stick, fork, or comb used to tightly pack weft threads.

heddle: a structure used to guide warp threads in a loom.

high-speed whorl: an option for inserting twist faster as you spin; usually smaller than standard whorls.

I

immersion dyeing: applying dye to fiber, yarn, or fabric in a water bath that includes the dyestuff and a fixative.

j

jack mechanism: a loom with a rising shed mechanism, in which shafts are either pulled or pushed up by jacks.

l

long draw: allowing the fiber hand to move in a long arc, drafting the fibers away from the spinning tool, wheel, or spindle.

loom: a tool upon which weaving is done.

loom waste: warp yarn left unwoven on the loom or used in tying on; the amount of a warp that cannot be woven.

m

mixed warp: a warp that includes two or more yarns of different fibers, twist amounts, or sizes; the warp yarns are intermingled in small groups or often end by end to counteract any potential shrinkage differences or finishing problems that may arise with using a variety of yarns in one warp.

mordant: a fixative used in dyeing to help set the color onto the fiber or yarn.

n

niddy-noddy: a tool used to wind skeins of yarn.

p

painted top: prepared top (fiber) that has been painted prior to spinning.

pick: one pass of the weft yarn.

picks per inch (ppi): the number of weft picks per inch in the fabric.

pin drafting: a mill process in which a roving is slighty attenuated to make a thinner preparation with better alignment.

plain weave: the simplest of weave structures, in which each weft yarn passes over every other warp yarn, alternating pick by pick.

plies: the number of strands used in a yarn construction. Singles are unplied yarns.

point of contact: the point at which fiber becomes yarn; where the twist begins to enter the fiber.

r

reed: a steel comb with teeth that space the warp; also used to press the weft in place. Reeds can also be made of bamboo or reed.

reed hook (also sley hook): a flat piece of metal, wood, or plastic with smooth curves at both ends for pulling threads through the dents of the reed.

roving: carded fiber; a step in the process of mechanical fiber preparation that is usually sold as a thick, ropelike continuous strand.

s

S-twist: the twist inserted when the wheel or spindle turns counterclockwise.

scotch tension: a system in which the drive wheel turns the flyer while the brake band slows the bobbin for winding on newly spun yarn.

selvedge: the edge on each side of a woven fabric where the weft turns around.

sett: the number of ends per inch (epi) in the warp.

shaft: a frame for holding the heddles on a loom.

shed: a space created between the warp threads and those lifted by the heddles, shed stick, or shafts.

shot (also pick): a woven row; one pass of the weft.

singles: the first product in spinning yarn; an unplied strand of yarn.

sizing: a surface preparation used to strengthen fibers during fabric construction; it is removable during the fabric finishing.

sley the reed: the process of placing the warp threads through the dents of the reed.

spaced-and-crammed warp: uneven threading of the warp in the reed; there may be empty spaces between groups of warps in the reed or some dents may have more than one warp, while some have fewer.

spin off the fold: the process of folding a bundle of fibers over the drafting forefinger and drafting from the side of the preparation; usually done with staple length sections of top or roving.

stick shuttle: flat piece of wood that is usually notched at each end so that the weft can be wrapped from end to end around the shuttle.

straight draw: threading the warp ends in order on the shafts: 1, 2, 3, 4 on a four-shaft loom or 1, 2, 3, 4, 5, 6, 7, 8 on an eight-shaft loom.

t

tabby: a weft that weaves plain weave when there is also another weft, usually heavier, that weaves pattern (as in overshot or summer and winter); sometimes used as a synonym for plain weave.

tablet weaving: using a set of four-holed tablets to hold the warps and create the weave structure also known as twining, or card weaving.

take-up: the amount of warp used up as it undulates over and under the weft threads; weave structures have more or less take-up; the size of the weft also affects the amount of take-up.

tentering: stretching a fabric under tension when drying; tentering frames have tenterhooks on which the newly washed fabric is stretched to dry.

threading: *(noun)* the order in which each warp end passes through a heddle on a specific shaft; *(verb)* inserting each warp end through a heddle.

threading hook (or heddle hook): a long, slender piece of flat metal with a handle at one end and a tight curve at the other to catch and pull warp threads through the heddles.

tie-up: a diagram that shows the shafts that must be raised and/or lowered by each treadle for a particular weave structure.

top: fiber that has been combed for uniformity in staple length and orientation.

tracking: movement of twist after the woven fabric is washed; appears on the surface of plain-weave fabrics as diagonal texture.

treadles: pedals on a loom that raise or lower the shafts to make the various sheds required by the weave structure.

treadling (also treadling order, treadling sequence): the order in which the treadles are depressed; i.e., the order in which each shed is made.

twist direction: denoted with Z for yarns spun with the wheel or spindle turning in a clockwise direction, and S for yarns spun with a wheel or spindle turning in the counterclockwise direction; the number of plies and the direction of plying is indicated as z2s (two Z-twist yarns plied in the S direction) or s2z (two S-twist yarns plied in the Z direction).

twists per inch (tpi): the number of times a yarn is twisted in an inch of length.

tying on: tying small groups of warp threads to the front or back apron rod.

W

warp: *(noun)* tensioned vertical or horizontal threads that form the base of a weaving; *(verb)* to string thread or yarn onto a loom.

warp-dominant: a fabric with more warp threads per inch than weft threads per inch in the cloth structure.

warp painting: directly applying (painting) dye to the warp chains before setting up the loom.

weave structure: the order in which warp and weft threads go over and under each other, i.e., the interlacement; if they interlace alternately, the weave structure is plain weave.

weft: threads or yarns that are woven across the warp; branches or grasses woven horizontally are also called weft.

weft-dominant: a fabric with more weft threads per inch than warp threads per inch in the cloth structure.

wheel ratio: the ratio between the drive wheel size and the whorl size, usually expressed numerically: 10:1 means that the whorl turns 10 times for every turn of the drive wheel.

whorl: the small wheel that drives either the flyer unit or the bobbin in a spinning wheel.

wraps per inch (wpi): the number of times a yarn can be wrapped consistently and loosely around a ruler or gauge within the space of an inch.

Y

yards per pound (ypp): the number of yards of yarn in one pound of weight; an indication of grist.

yarn blocker: a tool used to dry yarns under even, but not necessarily firm, tension.

Z

Z-twist: the twist inserted when the wheel or spindle turn clockwise.

resources
yarn AND *supplies*

A to Z Supply
13396 Ridge Rd.
Grass Valley, CA 95945
atozsupply.com
furniture-grade PVC parts

Abstract Fiber
3676 SE Martins St.
Portland, OR 97202
abstractfiber.com
dyed fiber, top, and roving

Ashland Bay
27501 SW 95th Ave., Ste. 970
Wilsonville, OR 97070
ashlandbay.com
wide selection of fibers

Brown Sheep Company
100662 County Rd. 16
Mitchell, NE 69357
brownsheep.com
yarn for warp or weft

Carin Engen
3750 Taylor Rd.
Loomis, CA 95650
thetinthimble.com/carinengen.html
dyed fibers

Carolina Homespun
455 Lisbon St.
San Francisco, CA 94112
carolinahomespun.com
fibers as well as spinning and weaving supplies

ColourMart
Unit 2A, Archers Wy.
Battlefield Ind Est
Shrewsbury SY1 3GA
United Kingdom
colourmart.com
weft yarns

Crown Mountain Farms
PO Box 2864
Yelm, WA 98597
crownmountainfarms.com
fibers and dyes

Denver Fabrics
2777 W. Belleview Ave.
Littleton, CO 80123
denverfabrics.com
fabrics for lining and interfacing

Gilmore Looms
1032 N. Broadway Ave.
Stockton, CA 95205
gilmorelooms.com
looms and weaving equipment

Henry's Attic
55 Mercury Ave.
Monroe, NY 10950
henrysattic.com
weft yarns

Lendrum
403 Millhaven Rd.
Odessa ON
Canada K0H 2H0
lendrum.ca
spinning wheels and equipment

Lola's Loom
19006 Summerland Ct.
Grass Valley, CA 95949
forsterherbgarden.com/wordpress
alpaca fiber

Morro Fleece Works
1920 Main St.
Morro Bay, CA 93442
morrofleeceworks.com
wide variety of fibers

Opulent Fiber
opulentfibers.com
luxury fibers

Portland Fiber Gallery & Weaving Studio
50 Cove St.
Portland, ME 04101
portlandfibergallery.com
spinning and weaving supplies and classes

Prochemical and Dye
126 Shove St.
Fall River, MA 02724
prochemicalanddye.com
dyes

Rainbow Farms Pygora
201 Wagner Rd.
Kelso, WA 98626
rfpygora.com
pygora fiber and yarn

Reflection Farm
31801-79th Ave. Ct. E.
Eatonville, WA 98328
reflectionfarm.net
pin-drafted dyed wool

Sakina Needles
This company is no longer in business.
alpaca roving

Schacht Spindle Company
6101 Ben Pl.
Boulder, CO 80301
schachtspindle.com
spinning wheels, looms, and spinning and
weaving equipment

Spinning Forth
Indie dyer in France
spinningforth.com
silk fibers and spinning and weaving tools

Spirit Trail Fiberworks
PO Box 197
Sperryville, VA 22740
spirit-trail.net
rare, endangered, and unusual breed fibers

Sweet Grass Wools
sweetgrasswool.com
dyed fiber top

The Spinning Loft
thespinningloft.com
fibers and spinning and weaving supplies

Treenway Silks
2060 Miller Ct.
Lakewood, CO 80215
treenwaysilks.com
natural and dyed silk threads, fibers, and yarns

Two Sisters Stringworks
twosistersstringworks.com
dyed fibers

Violet Linx
Indie dyer in Russia
violetlinx.etsy.com
dyed fibers and yarn

Yarn Chef
yarnchef.etsy.com
handpainted and hand-dyed yarns

Yarn Hollow
3041 Broadway SW
Grandville, MI 49418
yarnhollow.com
dyed fiber

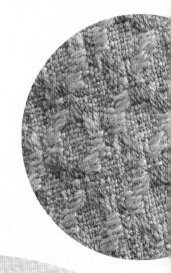

bibliography

TEXTILE TECHNIQUES

Amos, Alden. *The Alden Amos Big Book of Handspinning: Being a Compendium of Information, Advice, and Opinions on the Noble Art & Craft.* Loveland, Colorado: Interweave, 2001.

Baines, Patricia. *Spinning Wheels: Spinners and Spinning.* London: Batsford, 1977.

Casey, Maggie. *Start Spinning.* Loveland, Colorado: Interweave, 2008.

Chandler, Deborah. *Learning to Weave.* Loveland, Colorado: Interweave, 1995.

Davenport, Elsie G. *Your Handspinning.* New York: Select Books, 1978.

Hochberg, Bette. *Fibre Facts.* Santa Cruz, California: Hochberg, 1981.

—. *Handspindles.* Santa Cruz, California: B & B Hochberg, 1980.

—. *Handspinner's Handbook.* Santa Cruz, California: B & B Hochberg, 1976.

—. *Spin Span Spun: Facts and Folklore for Spinners and Weavers.* Santa Cruz, California: B & B Hochberg, 1979.

Lamb, Sara. *Woven Treasures.* Loveland, Colorado: Interweave, 2009.

Menz, Deb. *Color in Spinning.* Loveland, Colorado: Interweave, 2005.

—. *Color Works.* Loveland, Colorado: Interweave, 2004.

Robson, Deborah and Carol Ekarius. *The Fleece and Fiber Sourcebook.* North Adams, Massachusetts: Storey Publishing, 2011.

Ross, Mabel. *Essentials of Yarn Design for Handspinners.* Boston: Charles T. Branford, 1987.

—. *The Encyclopedia of Handspinning,* Loveland, Colorado: Interweave, 1988.

TEXTILE STUDY

Barber, Elizabeth Wayland. *Mummies of the Ürümchi.* New York: W. W. Norton & Company, 2000.

—. *Women's Work.* New York: W.W. Norton & Company, 1995.

Barber, E. J. W. *Prehistoric Textiles.* Princeton, NJ: Princeton University Press, 1992.

Ewing, Thor. *Viking Clothing.* Stroud, U.K.: Tempus, 2006.

Ostergaard, Else. *Woven into the Earth.* Aarhus, Denmark: Aarhus University Press, 2004.

Rogers, Penelope Walton. *Cloth and Clothing in Early Anglo-Saxon England, AD 450–700.* York, U.K.: Council for British Archaeology, 2007.

Weiner, Annette and Jane Schneider. *Cloth and Human Experience.* Washington, DC: Smithsonian Institution Press, 1991.

Wild, John Peter. *Textiles in Archaeology.* Oxford: Shire, 2008.

CLOTHING AND DESIGN

Burnham, Dorothy K. *Cut My Cote.* Toronto: Royal Ontario Museum, 1973.

Fransen, Lilli, Anna Norgaard, and Else Ostergaard. *Medieval Garments Reconstructed: Norse Clothing Patterns.* Aarhus, Denmark: Aarhus University Press, 2010.

Marshal, John. *Make Your Own Japanese Clothes: Patterns and Ideas for Modern Wear.* New York: Kodansha USA, 1988.

Mashuta, Mary. *Wearable Art for Real People.* Concord, California: C&T Publishing, 1989.

Mayer, Anita. *Clothing from the Hands that Weave.* Loveland, Colorado: Interweave, 1984.

Tilke, Max. *Costume Patterns and Designs.* New York: Hastings House, 1974.

¾" *pvc yarn*
blocker

MATERIALS

You will need 16 feet (4.9 m) of ¾" (2 cm) PVC pipe cut into the following lengths:

* *six 10" (25.5 cm) lengths for blocking surface*

* *fourteen 6" (15 cm) lengths for arms, handle, and short sides of base*

* *two 16" (40.5 cm) lengths for long sides of base*

* *two 3" (7.5 cm) lengths for axles*

You will also need the following parts:

* *fourteen 90° elbow-joints*

* *two T-joints*

* *two end-caps*

* *two slip-joints (available as furniture-grade PVC part)*

* *two 5-way connectors (available as furniture-grade PVC part)*

ASSEMBLY

BASE: Assemble the base with two 16" (40.5 cm) lengths, four 6" (15 cm) lengths, four elbow-joints, and two T-joints. Glue all joins with PVC glue.

Glue one 10" (25.5 cm) length into each of two T-joints, top each with a slip-joint, then glue all in place, orienting the slip-joint so that the opening faces the center of the blocker.

AXLE: Insert a 3" (7.5 cm) length into each slip-joint for the axle but do not glue—the blocker must turn freely on this axle.

Glue an end-cap to the outside end of one 3" (7.5 cm) length piece, making sure the slip-joint turns freely.

HANDLE: Attach one elbow-joint to the outside end of the other 3" (7.5 cm) length, attach one 6" (15 cm) length to the other end of the elbow-joint, then attach another elbow-joint to the open end. Glue in place.

Attach another 6" (15 cm) length to the open elbow-joint and finish off with an end-cap. Glue in place, making sure that the axle turns freely.

REEL: Attach four 6" (15 cm) lengths to the four arms of each 5-way connector. Glue in place.

Glue an elbow-joint to the end of each arm.

Slip the 5-way connectors onto the 3" (7.5 cm) axles. Carefully glue in place, being careful that no glue gets into the slip-joint and that the axle turns freely.

Attach four 10" (25.5 cm) lengths between the elbows to connect the arms. Glue in place.

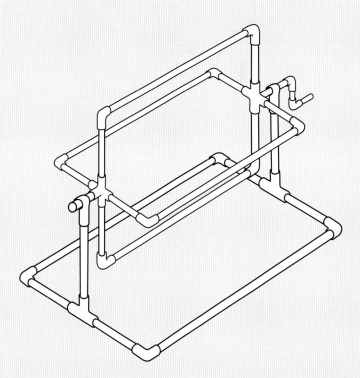

kimono
assembly

Begin with finished fabric that measures 18" (45.5 cm) wide and 168" (427 cm) long.

NOTE: *If you want to weave the front band separately, begin with a finished width of 14" to 15" (35.5 to 38 cm) and weave the band 6" (15 cm) wide and 168" (427 cm) long.*

Cut the fabric into pieces as shown in the cutting diagram on page 139.

Cut out a teardrop-shape neckline from each body piece so that the opening begins 1" (2.5 cm) to the back of the shoulder line, measures 4" (10 cm) wide at the shoulder line, and is 15" (38 cm) long in total. Machine serge or zigzag the cut edge.

Fold and press each body piece to mark the halfway point of each length (this corresponds to the shoulder line).

Sew the left front/back to the right front/back for 26" (66 cm), or 1" (2.5 cm) below the halfway point, for the back seam. Press seam allowance open.

Lay garment flat and mark a point at least 8¼" (21 cm) down from the shoulder line on front. Beginning at marked point, pin sleeve to body so that it extends 8" (20.5 cm) to the front of the shoulder line. Sew in place, using a ½" (1.3 cm) seam allowance and leaving ½" (1.3 cm) unsewn at front edge. Press seam allowance open.

Fold back sleeve along the diagonal, matching Points A and B and aligning the sections from A to B on the front of the sleeve. With right sides facing together and using the ¼" (6 mm) unsewn section on the front as a guide, sew in place. Press seam allowance open.

Sew front sleeve to body front. Sew front to back along sides toward hemline, leaving a vent at the lower body, if desired.

Turn under selvedge at cuff and sew in place.

Turn up hemline, allowing for the desired amount of facing, and sew in place.

Fold neckband in half lengthwise and sew raw edges around neck opening, from hem to hem. Topstitch if desired.

Add buttons, ties, etc., as desired.

Form one large pleat or two or three small pleats at shoulders to pull in extra fabric and allow the hem to hang straight. Topstitch in place for 16" to 20" (40.5 to 51 cm) across shoulder from back to front.

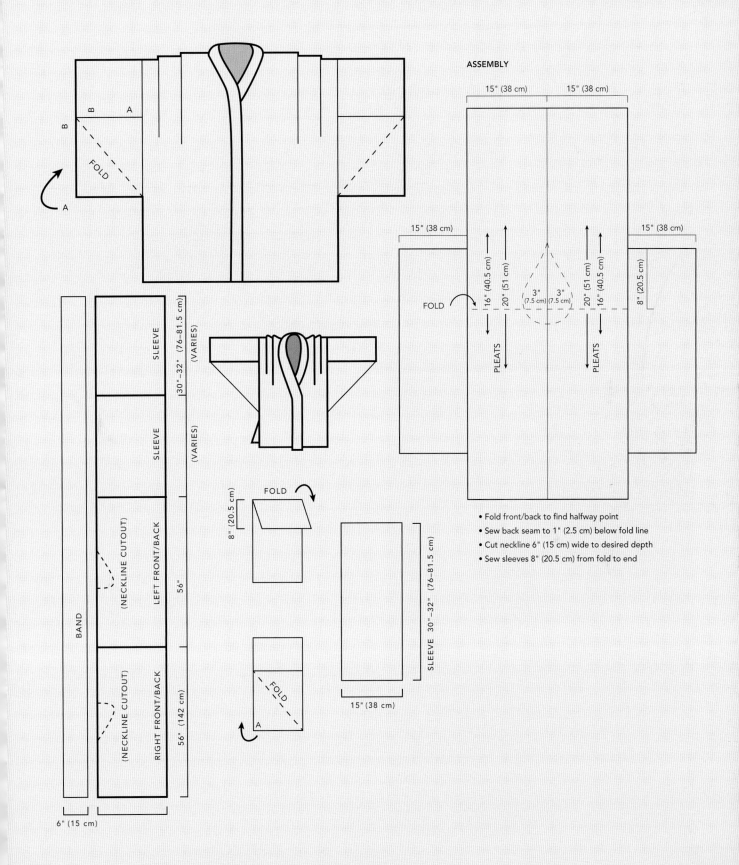

ASSEMBLY

15" (38 cm)   15" (38 cm)

15" (38 cm)

16" (40.5 cm)   20" (51 cm)

3" (7.5 cm)   3" (7.5 cm)

20" (51 cm)   16" (40.5 cm)

15" (38 cm)

8" (20.5 cm)

FOLD

PLEATS

PLEATS

• Fold front/back to find halfway point
• Sew back seam to 1" (2.5 cm) below fold line
• Cut neckline 6" (15 cm) wide to desired depth
• Sew sleeves 8" (20.5 cm) from fold to end

B   B   A

B

FOLD

A

BAND

(NECKLINE CUTOUT)

LEFT FRONT/BACK

SLEEVE

SLEEVE

(VARIES)

30"–32" (76–81.5 cm)

(VARIES)

56"

(NECKLINE CUTOUT)

RIGHT FRONT/BACK

56" (142 cm)

6" (15 cm)

8" (20.5 cm)

FOLD

FOLD

A

SLEEVE   30"–32" (76–81.5 cm)

15" (38 cm)

tibetan jacket
assembly

Begin with finished fabric that measures 18" (45.5 cm) wide and 6.2 yd (5.7 m) long.

Cut the fabric into pieces as shown in the cutting diagram on page 141.

Fold and press each body piece to mark the halfway point of each length (this corresponds to the shoulder line).

Sew the left front/back to the right front/back for 26" (66 cm), or 1" (2.5 cm) below the shoulder line, for the back seam. Press seam open.

Cut out a round neckline that begins at the top of the back seam 1" (2.5 cm) below the shoulder line, measures 8" (21.5 cm) wide at the shoulder line, and extends 5" (12.5 cm) to the front of the shoulder line. Machine surge or zigzag the cut edge.

Sew pockets onto lower edge of each front so that tops of pockets are even across the center front opening.

Fold tucks at shoulders and lower body as necessary for desired fit and stitch in place along the entire length of the tucks.

Sew the two sleeve pieces together along the long edge, then cut the seamed piece on the diagonal as shown to form the two sleeves.

Sew the wide edge of each sleeve to the body, centering the sleeves at the shoulder line so that the lower edges meet at the sides.

Sew side and sleeve seams.

Cut off 4" to 5" (10 to 12.5 cm)—enough so that your wrist and hand will slide through comfortably—from each sleeve point to create the cuff edge.

Sew cuff bands to sleeves, aligning raw edges. Fold band to the inside and sew in place. Topstitch if desired.

Turn under selvedge along front edges to make facings and sew in place.

With right sides facing together, sew waistband to lower edge, matching raw edges and adding tucks as necessary for the desired fit. Fold band to the inside and sew in place. Topstitch if desired.

Sew collar band to neck opening as for sleeve cuffs.

Add five to seven buttonholes as desired, placing one in the collar band, one near the hemline, and the others evenly spaced in between. Sew buttons to left front, opposite buttonholes, so that the fronts overlap at least 1" (2.5 cm).

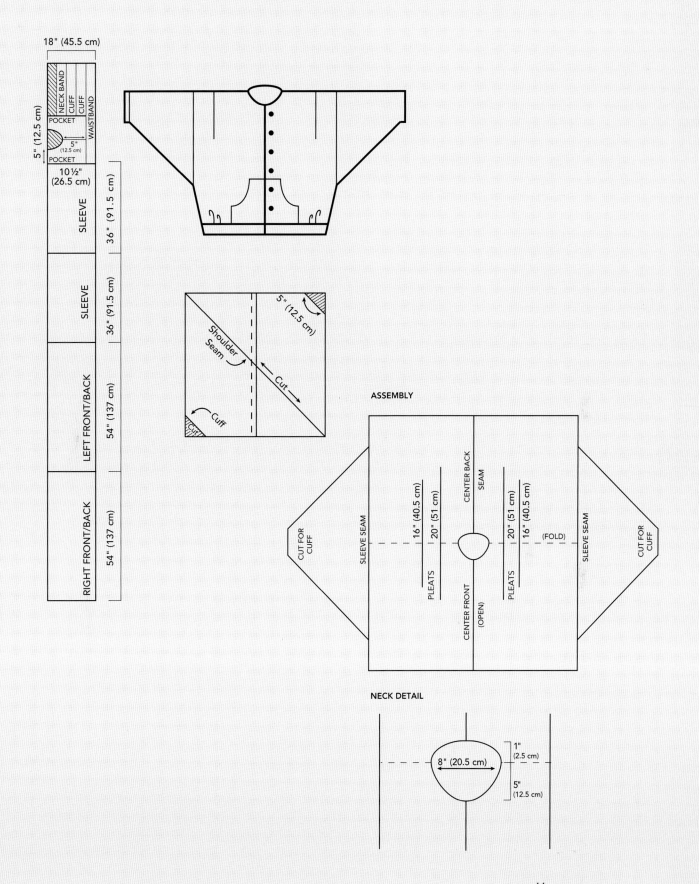

18" (45.5 cm)

5" (12.5 cm)

NECK BAND

CUFF

CUFF

WAISTBAND

POCKET

5"
(12.5 cm)

POCKET

10½"
(26.5 cm)

SLEEVE   36" (91.5 cm)

SLEEVE   36" (91.5 cm)

LEFT FRONT/BACK   54" (137 cm)

RIGHT FRONT/BACK   54" (137 cm)

5" (12.5 cm)

Shoulder Seam

Cut

Cuff

Cuff

ASSEMBLY

CUT FOR CUFF

SLEEVE SEAM

16" (40.5 cm)

20" (51 cm)

CENTER BACK

SEAM

20" (51 cm)

16" (40.5 cm)

(FOLD)

SLEEVE SEAM

CUT FOR CUFF

PLEATS

PLEATS

CENTER FRONT

(OPEN)

NECK DETAIL

1"
(2.5 cm)

8" (20.5 cm)

5"
(12.5 cm)

spinning and weaving ∾ RECORD SHEET

DATE: .... PROJECT: ....

FIBER: .... *source:* ....

.... *prep:* .... *amount:* ....

DATE: .... PROJECT: ....

FIBER: .... *source:* ....

.... *prep:* .... *amount:* ....

DATE: .... PROJECT: ....

FIBER: .... *source:* ....

.... *prep:* .... *amount:* ....

spinning details: WARP YARN(S)

EQUIPMENT USED: ....

YARN 1: .... *fiber:* .... *# plies:* .... *direction of plies:* ....

.... *tpi/wpi/ypp:* ....

YARN 2: .... *fiber:* .... *# plies:* .... *direction of plies:* ....

.... *tpi/wpi/ypp:* ....

YARN 3: .... *fiber:* .... *# plies:* .... *direction of plies:* ....

.... *tpi/wpi/ypp:* ....

dyeing details

....

....

weaving details

EQUIPMENT USED: ....

sett: .... *width of warp:* .... *length of warp:* .... *# of ends:* ....

weft: .... *ppi:* ....

FINISHING: ....

yarn and fabric details:

....

....

index

Fill your library with these inspirational
~ *weaving resources from Interweave*

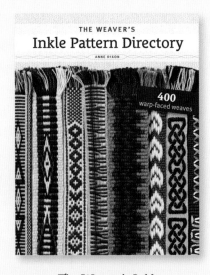

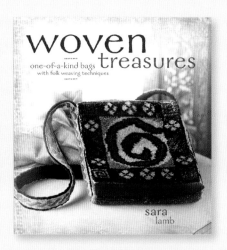

*The Weaver's Inkle
Pattern Directory*
400 WARP-FACED WEAVES
Anne Dixon
ISBN 978-1-59668-647-2
$29.95

Woven Treasures
ONE-OF-A-KIND BAGS WITH
FOLK WEAVING TECHNIQUES
Sara Lamb
ISBN 978-1-59668-102-6
$24.95

Color and Texture in Weaving
150 CONTEMPORARY DESIGNS
Margo Selby
ISBN 978-1-59668-372-3
$26.95

WEAVING TODAY. SHOP
SHOP.WEAVINGTODAY.COM

HANDWOVEN.

Handwoven is the premiere resource for everyone
interested in weaving, from beginners to seasoned
professionals. Each issue introduces you to weavers
from around the world and is filled with tips and tricks
of the trade, the latest tools, and you'll be among the
first to know about new innovations or creative ideas.
Weavingtoday.com

WEAVING TODAY.

Weaving Today is the town square for handweavers
and the online community for *Handwoven* magazine.
Weavingtoday.com

CPSIA information can be obtained
at www.ICGtesting.com
Printed in the USA
BVHW021518030620
580777BV00004B/175